ROOSEVELT HOUSE
AT HUNTER COLLEGE

The Story of
Franklin and Eleanor's
New York City Home

When the house on 65th Street was completed in 1908, Franklin and Eleanor had two children, Anna and James. (Courtesy of the Franklin D. Roosevelt Library Digital Archives)

ROOSEVELT HOUSE
AT HUNTER COLLEGE

The Story of
Franklin and Eleanor's
New York City Home

Text by
DEBORAH S. GARDNER

Foreword by
JENNIFER J. RAAB

Compiled and edited by
JAMES G. BASKER,
JUSTINE AHLSTROM, ELAINE BLEAKNEY,
SHEILA FUENTES, AND NICOLE SEARY

THE GILDER LEHRMAN
INSTITUTE *of* AMERICAN HISTORY
&
HUNTER
The City University of New York

New York • 2009

Produced for

ROOSEVELT
HOUSE

PUBLIC POLICY INSTITUTE
AT HUNTER COLLEGE

47–49 EAST 65TH STREET
NEW YORK, NY 10065
www.roosevelthouse.hunter.cuny.edu

by

THE GILDER LEHRMAN
INSTITUTE *of* AMERICAN HISTORY
19 WEST 44TH STREET, SUITE 500
NEW YORK, NY 10036
www.gilderlehrman.org

CONTENTS

FOREWORD

Roosevelt House—the magnificent double townhouse on East 65th Street that was the New York City home of Franklin and Eleanor Roosevelt, as well as Franklin's mother, Sara—is a vital part of the history of New York City and the nation. It is where FDR recovered from polio, where he celebrated the evening he learned he would be president, and where Eleanor began her unparalleled career as an advocate for human rights and social justice. We at Hunter College are proud to be an important part of that history. The Roosevelts were more than simply neighbors of Hunter College, located only blocks away on East 68th Street. As was characteristic of their belief in the power of education to transform society, they became actively involved in the life of the college, as beloved campus visitors and valuable mentors to a generation of students. The Roosevelts changed many of those students' lives and left a long-lasting influence at Hunter that continues to this day—now more than ever, as we celebrate Roosevelt House's long-awaited reopening.

The special relationship between Hunter College and the Roosevelts was fortified when, following Sara's death in 1941, the Roosevelts arranged for Hunter to purchase the house the next year; Franklin wrote the first check himself, for $1,000. Eleanor spoke at the Hunter commencement ceremony in 1942 as well as at the dedication ceremony when the house opened in 1943. Named "the Sara Delano Roosevelt Interfaith Memorial House," the house became the nation's first interfaith college center, a place where students of all religious backgrounds could come together to share ideas and foster mutual understanding. The Roosevelts were deeply supportive of what, at the time, was a truly ground-breaking initiative. In a letter that Eleanor read at the dedication in 1943, FDR expressed his wish that "this movement for tolera-tion . . . grow and prosper until there is a similar establishment in every institution of higher learning in the land."

And indeed, Roosevelt House flourished as a vibrant student center and important cultural institution at Hunter for many years—not to mention a wedding hall of choice for many a Hunter bride. Sadly, in 1992, Hunter was compelled to close the house due to deterioration and safety concerns. It stood unused for over a decade, until we were able to begin the gratifying and exciting task of restoring the house and bringing it back into the life and landscape of Hunter College.

The years-long restoration was an enormous undertaking—but thanks to the ongoing dedication and foresight of CUNY Chancellor Matthew Goldstein and the entire CUNY leadership team, the project has been a resounding success. We are grateful to the many New York public figures and private individuals who have made the restoration possible. We have been particularly in-spired by the wisdom and enthusiasm of our friend Ambassador William J. vanden Heuvel, whose steadfast commitment to preserving the Roosevelt legacy has guided us in every step of the process. Thanks also to Polshek Partnership Architects, who achieved the perfect balance between faithful restoration and twenty-first-century functionality.

The physical restoration was just the beginning, however. It was also apparent that this historic property should serve to commemorate the Roosevelts and honor their legacy in a way that would benefit not just the college, but the community at large. We could think of no better way of doing so than making it the home of the new Public Policy Institute at Hunter College, where students, scholars, journalists, politicians, and leaders in every field can come together to teach, learn, discuss and develop policies to better our world.

From the beginning, one of our primary goals has been to share the fascinating story of Roosevelt House and to ensure that future generations have access to this piece of American history. We are proud that the House will be open to the public for tours, as well as the many events sponsored by the Public Policy Institute. And of course, this book, ably written by historian Dr. Deborah Gardner, will serve as an irreplaceable record, sure to be added to the list of essential readings about Franklin and Eleanor. Its publication would not have been possible without the great generosity of Richard Gilder and Lewis Lehrman, co-founders of the Gilder Lehrman Institute of American History, and the Institute's president, Dr. James Basker.

Like the house itself, this book is a tribute to all that Franklin and Eleanor shared with Hunter College. I believe that the Roosevelts saw their dreams reflected in Hunter, which was founded on a commitment to education and opportunity for all, regardless of class, race, ethnicity, or gender. Every day, on one of the most diverse campuses in the nation, we renew our commitment to making the American Dream come true. In the process, we are constantly reminded of the legacy of the Roosevelts, and we are proud of Hunter College's role in carrying that legacy forward.

Again, we owe the privilege in doing so to the incredible support and involvement of the City University of New York's brilliant and far-thinking chancellor, Dr. Matthew Goldstein. Roosevelt House is just one more piece of evidence attesting to the revitalization CUNY has experienced under Chancellor Goldstein's incomparable leadership. We also owe sincere gratitude to the entire CUNY administration and Board of Trustees, starting with Executive Vice Chancellor Allan Dobrin and Vice-Chancellor for Facilities Iris Weinshall, without whose support this project would never have seen the light of day.

I invite you to visit Roosevelt House and to take part in the next chapter of its storied history.

JENNIFER J. RAAB
President, Hunter College

INTRODUCTION

⟋

Franklin Delano Roosevelt was the most transformative president of the twentieth century. His wife, Eleanor, was the most consequential First Lady—and one of the most consequential women of her time. Each was a child of privilege, but the impact of their upbringing could not have been more different.

The Roosevelts were among the oldest and most prominent families in New York City. The first members of the American clan, Claes Martenzen van Roosevelt and his wife, Jannetje, had arrived aboard a vessel from Holland sometime before 1648. (His name, translated from Dutch into English means "Nicholas, son of Martin, of the Rose Field."[1]) Eight generations of their descendants had built sizable fortunes as importers of window glass and West Indian sugar, as bankers, and as dealers in Manhattan real estate. Most of the early Roosevelts lived near the southern tip of Manhattan Island but they moved steadily northward with other descendants of New York's first settlers as immigrants from elsewhere turned the tiny Dutch village they'd known into an

Seventeen-year-old Franklin Roosevelt poses with his parents, James and Sara Delano Roosevelt, in May 1899. Eighteen months later, Franklin came home from his first semester at Harvard College to be with his dying father. (Courtesy of the Franklin D. Roosevelt Library Digital Archives)

Franklin's father, James, purchased Springwood in 1867. The 110-acre estate included a farmhouse, parts of which dated to 1800. James, and later Sara and Franklin, would add on and renovate the original building to create a roomy Federal-style mansion. Franklin donated the estate to the American people, and today it is a national historic site. (Library of Congress Prints and Photographs Division)

ever-more-crowded city. By 1901, Theodore Roosevelt, Eleanor's uncle and Franklin's cousin, was president of the United States.

Franklin was born in 1882 at Hyde Park, New York. His father, James Roosevelt, was a some-time attorney and businessman, and full-time country gentleman. His mother, Sara Delano Roosevelt, then about half her husband's age, was regal, self-assured, and single-mindedly devoted to her only child. Their boy was brought up to be stoical, to consider it his duty to help those less fortunate than he, and to believe that he could succeed at anything to which he put his hand. His mother's fond but sometimes intrusive interest in the most minute details of his life also taught him the creative uses of charm and misdirection.

Franklin's youth armed him with self-confidence. Eleanor's girlhood was sad and less secure. She was born in 1884. Her mother, Anna Hall Roosevelt, beautiful and self-absorbed, made it clear that she found her young daughter disappointingly plain. Eleanor's mostly absentee father was Theodore Roosevelt's

Elliott Roosevelt, younger brother of Theodore Roosevelt, poses here in 1892 with his daughter Eleanor and two sons (Gracie Hall, known as Hall, in his lap and Elliott Jr., at far right). The children's mother, Anna Hall Roosevelt, had died from diphtheria that year, and Elliott Jr. succumbed to the same disease in 1893. A year later, Eleanor and Hall were orphaned upon the death of their father. (Courtesy of the Franklin D. Roosevelt Library Digital Archives)

alcoholic brother, Elliott. Eleanor was orphaned at ten, and raised by relatives who were dutiful rather than loving.

Franklin attended Groton School in Massachusetts and was at Harvard when he began secretly courting his distant cousin, Eleanor. She had just returned from three years in England at the Allenswood School, where she had developed some social confidence and made friends. The couple was engaged in 1904 and married the following year.

Like a good many members of their class, they divided their time among several residences. Most summers were spent on Campobello Island in Canadian waters off the coast of Maine, where Franklin and his parents had typically summered. And for as many weeks as possible during the spring and autumn the family moved to Springwood (which was always referred to simply as "Hyde Park"), his mother's country place at Hyde Park, New York, where he'd been born and brought up. Like his father, FDR always saw himself as a country gentleman; and as late as 1944, living in the White House and having been elected president of the United States four times, he still enjoyed listing his occupation as "tree grower."[2] In New York City, Franklin and Eleanor shared a common wall with Sara Delano Roosevelt in the twin townhouse she had had built for them in 1908 on East 65th Street. Despite the time split between country and city residences, the Roosevelts' New York City home nonetheless witnessed more than its share of history and at least as much personal struggle and sorrow as political triumph.

Franklin was elected to the New York State Senate as a Democrat in 1910, which took him and the family to Albany for the legislative session in 1911. They were back in New York in the autumn of 1912 when both Roosevelts fell ill with typhoid fever. Franklin lay in his upstairs bedroom for weeks, worried because he was unable actively to campaign for reelection, while his aide Louis McHenry Howe canvassed Dutchess County in his place. Howe helped win the race for his boss and then won for himself a permanent spot as FDR's most important advisor. Howe's eccentricities—he smoked ceaselessly, rarely bathed or laundered his clothes, turned up at the house at odd hours—made him unpopular at first with everyone else in the family, but without his shrewd counsel and fierce loyalty, Franklin Roosevelt might never have become president.

Franklin then served seven years as Assistant Secretary of the Navy in Washington, where he learned how government worked and Eleanor made her first tentative steps toward independence, working as a Red Cross volunteer during World War I. Her 1918 discovery of her husband's romance with her social secretary,

Eleanor (right), at age twenty, with her future mother-in-law, Sara, in 1904 at the Roosevelts' summer home in Campobello, New Brunswick, a few months before Franklin and Eleanor announced their engagement. (Courtesy of the Franklin D. Roosevelt Library Digital Archives)

Lucy Mercer, taught her never again to rely on anyone else for her own fulfillment. The Roosevelts would remain married for the sake of their children and his political career, and they eventually formed one of the most effective political partnerships in history, but she would never again merely be his help-mate.

Roosevelt ran for vice president in 1920 and lost, then returned to New York again so that he could travel to and from his new office at Broadway and Chambers Street. There, as vice president of the Fidelity & Deposit Company of Maryland, a large surety bonding concern, he did what he called mostly "glad-hand stuff" while plotting a return to politics.[3]

Then, at Campobello in August 1921, disaster struck. Franklin contracted infantile paralysis, or poliomyelitis, at the unusually late age of thirty-nine, and the disease robbed him of the use of his legs. Returning to New York, he spent six weeks in Presbyterian Hospital on East 68th Street and then found himself being carried into the New York City house, all the way up to a quiet back bedroom on the third floor. Eleanor Roosevelt remembered the New York winter of 1921–22 as "in many ways the most trying . . . of my entire life."[4] That was surely an understatement.

Doctors came and went. So did friends and well-wishers, nannies and servants, and worried relatives. Newspapermen knocked on the door and had gently to be fended off: no one was to be told how ill Roosevelt had been or how badly his legs had been affected for fear the news would end his career. Physical therapists put him through agonizing stretching exercises to which his mother strenuously objected. "My mother-in-law thought we were tiring my husband," Eleanor remembered. "She always thought that she understood what was best, particularly where her child was concerned, regardless of what any doctor might say."[5] The arguments between his wife and mother eventually added so much to the patient's own anxiety about his condition that when spring came his doctors would successfully urge him to shift out of his crowded Manhattan house for a time to the relative serenity of Hyde Park.

His children were anxious, too, and Roosevelt did his gallant best to allay their fears. "He apparently knew it would be a shock for us to realize that the useless muscles in his legs would cause atrophy," his daughter, Anna, recalled. "So Father removed the sadness by showing us his legs. He gave us the names of each of the muscles in them, then told us which ones he was working

Franklin and his two oldest sons, James and Elliott, show off ship models at Campobello in 1920. Stricken with polio there in 1921, Franklin would return to the summer home for only three short visits in the 1930s. (Hunter College)

hardest on at that moment. He would shout with glee over a little movement of a muscle that had been dormant. . . . The battle Father was making became a spirited game."[6]

He would lose that game, of course: he was never able to walk unaided. But the contest that began that winter in the house on 65th Street would bring out in him qualities not before much in evidence during his largely charmed life—patience, application, recognition of his own limitations, a willingness to fail in front of others and try again—qualities that would help him face and overcome the two worst crises of the twentieth century.

FDR became governor of New York in 1928, and was elected president for the first time in 1932. (He would run again and win in 1936, 1940 and 1944.) Only a handful of presidents have found themselves facing the kind of crisis that truly tests their leadership.

May 30, 1934

FOR THE PRESS

323

CONFIDENTIAL UNTIL RELEASED

CAUTION: This address of the President at Gettysburg, Pennsylvania, today, May 30, 1934, MUST BE HELD FOR RELEASE and no portion, synopsis or intimation is to be published or given out until its delivery has actually begun.
CAUTION: Care must be exercised to avoid premature publication.

STEPHEN EARLY
Assistant Secretary to the President

GETTYSBURG ADDRESS

My Friends:

On these hills of Gettysburg two brave armies of Americans once met in combat. Not far from here, in a valley likewise consecrated to American valor, a ragged Continental Army survived a bitter winter to keep alive the expiring hope of a new Nation; and near to this battle-field and that valley stands that invincible city where the Declaration of Independence was born and the Constitution of the United States was written by the fathers. Surely, all this is holy ground.

It was in Philadelphia, too, that Washington spoke his solemn, tender, wise words of farewell -- a farewell not alone to his generation, but to the generation of those who laid down their lives here and to our generation and to the America of tomorrow. Perhaps if our fathers and grandfathers had truly heeded those words we should have had no family quarrel, no battle of Gettysburg, no Appomattox.

As a Virginian, President Washington had a natural pride in Virginia; but as an American, in his stately phrase, "the name of American, which belongs to you, in your National capacity, must always exalt the just pride of Patriotism, more than any appellation derived from local discrimination."

Recognizing the strength of local and State and sectional pre-judices and how strong they might grow to be, and how they might take from the National Government some of the loyalty the citizens owed to it, he made three historic tours during his Presidency. One was through New England in 1789, another through the Northern States in 1790, and still another through the Southern States in 1791. He did this, as he said, "In order to become better acquainted with their principal characters and internal circumstances, as well as to be more accessible to numbers of well informed persons who might give him useful advices on political subjects."

But he did more to stimulate patriotism than merely to travel and mingle with the people. He knew that Nations grow as their commerce and manufactures and agriculture grow, and that all of these grow as the means of transportation are extended. He sought to knit the sections to gether by their common interest in these great enterprises; and he pro-jected highways and canals as aids not to sectional, but to national development.

Invited to speak at Gettysburg in 1934, President Roosevelt shrewdly avoided any comparison with Lincoln's famous speech of November 1863 by shifting his focus to the heroism of George Washington and his troops at Valley Forge. Roosevelt invokes Washington as a proponent of canals, highways, and other national infrastructure to place FDR's own New Deal program of public works in the light of historic precedent. (Gilder Lehrman Collection)

FDR signed the U.S. declaration of war against Germany on December 11, 1941, four days after Japan attacked Pearl Harbor, thrusting the United States into World War II. (Library of Congress Prints and Photographs Division)

FDR faced two: the Great Depression and the Second World War. On the domestic front, he would do more to alter the old relationship between ordinary citizens and their government than any other president. Before Roosevelt and his New Deal, there was no unemployment compensation or Social Security; no regulation of the stock market; no federal guarantee of bank deposits or the right to bargain; no minimum wage or maximum hours; no federal commitment to equal opportunity or high employment. In the struggle to achieve these and other reforms Eleanor Roosevelt was the President's tireless partner, traveling the country to see how government programs were working on the ground, drumming up support in her newspaper column, "My Day," and often prodding her husband to act still more boldly from behind the scenes.

The United States emerged from the World War II the most powerful nation in the world. Many factors contributed to that result but Roosevelt's refusal to be intimidated by tyrants and his belief that he and his country would prevail whatever the odds were crucial. Again, his wife played an important part, her reform agenda expanding to encompass much of the world.

FDR's death in 1945 meant Eleanor Roosevelt could no longer affect policy directly, but she remained a powerful figure until the end of her life in 1962. She championed civil rights and civil liberties, and, as U.S. delegate to the United Nations and chair of its Human Rights Commission, won passage of the Universal Declaration of Human Rights. She, as much as Franklin, had claimed her own place in history.

Courtesy of The Gilder Lehrman Institute of American History

ENDNOTES

1 Nathan Miller, *The Roosevelt Chronicles* (Garden City, NY: Doubleday, 1979), 4.
2 Geoffrey C. Ward, *A First-Class Temperament: The Emergence of Franklin Roosevelt* (New York: Harper & Row, 1989), 121*n*.
3 Ward, *A First-Class Temperament*, 562.
4 Eleanor Roosevelt, *This Is My Story* (New York: Harper & Brothers, 1937), 336.
5 Eleanor Roosevelt, *The Autobiography of Eleanor Roosevelt* (New York: Da Capo, 1992), 117–18.
6 John R. Boettiger, *A Love in Shadow* (New York: W.W. Norton, 1978), 89.

A DYNAMIC LIFE: THE ROOSEVELTS ON EAST 65TH STREET, 1908–1942

The story of Roosevelt House begins with the marriage of Franklin Roosevelt and his distant cousin Anna Eleanor Roosevelt (who was always called Eleanor). The marriage reunited two branches of the Roosevelt family, the Oyster Bay Roosevelts, led by Eleanor's grandfather, Theodore Roosevelt Sr., and the Hudson River Roosevelts, led by Franklin's father, James Roosevelt. James had married Sara Delano in 1880, and when he died in 1900 at the age of 72, their only child, Franklin, was 18 years old. He had a much older half brother, James "Rosy" Roosevelt Roosevelt, from his father's first marriage.

Franklin and Eleanor began seeing each other soon after she returned from school in England in 1902 to make her social debut. They discussed marriage in 1903, but, as Franklin would not graduate from Harvard College until June 1904, and Sara thought the couple was too young to marry, the engagement and the wedding were put off for a year. While Franklin finished his schooling, Eleanor joined the Consumers League to investigate

An elegant and pensive Eleanor poses in her wedding gown in 1905. The New York Times *described her as "a very slight and very tall figure, a handsome young woman of much charm." The lace had been worn by her maternal grandmother; her bridal veil belonged to her godmother, Susan Parish; and her pearl collar necklace was from Sara Roosevelt. (Courtesy of the Franklin D. Roosevelt Library Digital Archives)*

working conditions in low-income jobs and volunteered at the Rivington Settlement House, teaching the children of immigrants, following a family tradition of assisting the poor. Her experiences provided her with the firsthand knowledge of poverty that would influence her in later years.

After graduating from Harvard, Franklin enrolled in Columbia Law School in September 1904. He and Eleanor announced their engagement at Thanksgiving and set the wedding for the following spring. President Theodore Roosevelt, Eleanor's uncle, sent his congratulations to Franklin: "I am as fond of Eleanor as if she were my daughter," and offered the couple a White House wedding. They declined, preferring to marry in New York.[1]

The ceremony took place on March 17, 1905 at the Ludlow-Parish house at 6–8 East 76th Street, the home of Eleanor's cousin and godmother, Susan Parish. Theodore Roosevelt was in New York to attend the St. Patrick's Day parade and to give the bride away. A note in the *New York Times'* society pages captured the spirit of the event: "The wedding of Miss Eleanor Roosevelt and Franklin Delano Roosevelt, her cousin, took the semblance of a National event. The presence of President Roosevelt . . . and the entire family in every degree of cousinship made it very much like a 'royal alliance' . . . The President is never so happy as when he is one of the chief actors in a great family gathering."[2] The young couple spent a week at Hyde Park, deferring their honeymoon in Europe until the summer so that Franklin could finish his semester at law school.

At Christmastime in 1905, when the couple had been married less than a year, Sara promised her son and daughter-in-law a new home. She gave them a sketch of a single townhouse with a note that said, "number & street not yet quite decided — 19 or 20 feet wide." Sara had received a considerable fortune from her husband's estate, which, along with an inheritance from her own

In 1905, Sara Delano Roosevelt gave her son and daughter-in-law this note
with the promise of a house. (Courtesy of the Franklin D. Roosevelt Library
Digital Archives)

family, comfortably continued to support her upper-class lifestyle. She and the young couple were then living within a few blocks of one another in the Murray Hill section of Manhattan in the East 30s, where families of old wealth had settled in the 1880s and 1890s. Sara had not yet purchased a lot nor chosen plans for the house. As nearby blocks drew commercial development, Mrs. Roosevelt determined to move uptown to a more residential neighborhood. The Upper East Side, which ran from the East 50s through the East 80s and filled the blocks between Fifth and Lexington Avenues, was her destination, close to family and friends.

In early 1907, Mrs. Roosevelt bought two properties on the north side of East 65th Street between Park and Madison Avenues and recorded in her diary on January 11, "I drove Franklin up to see 47 and 49 East 65th Street." She had paid $79,000 for the land and two four-story brownstones built in 1876. Sara had them both demolished, an act that reflected the era's disenchantment with the ubiquitous brownstone-faced row house.[3]

Mrs. Roosevelt decided that she would construct one building that would contain two residences, one for herself, and one for Franklin and Eleanor. Her model was the Ludlow-Parish house where Franklin and Eleanor were married. Susan Ludlow Parish and her husband, banker Henry Parish Jr., shared the building with Susan's mother. It looked like one building from the outside, but behind the common street wall there were two separate units. Eleanor had lived there during the winter when she made her debut, so Sara knew that Eleanor and Franklin were familiar with the dual-family arrangement.

Architect Charles A. Platt was hired to design the house. He was a successful designer of city houses and suburban estates for elite clients and had remodeled brownstones for the Astor Estate Office, where Rosy Roosevelt worked. Rosy may have influenced

Architect Charles Platt

Platt in Paris, c. 1885. (Avery Architectural & Fine Arts Library, Columbia University)

Charles A. Platt (1861–1933) was born, raised, and educated in New York City. He studied drawing and painting at the National Academy of Design and the Art Students League. By 1880, he had also learned how to etch from Philadelphia artist Stephen Parrish (father of the noted illustrator Maxfield Parrish) and exhibited his first etchings to acclaim. But Platt, like many other young American artists, felt that he needed additional training and departed in 1882 for Europe. For five years he studied painting, continued etching, and took courses in architecture. He returned to America in 1887 with basic drafting skills and a knowledge of historical styles.

Platt settled in New York to pursue his career as an artist. Two years later he was introduced to Cornish, New Hampshire, where many artists and literary figures gathered each summer. He loved the landscape there, bought land in 1890, and built a house and gardens. Soon Platt was embarked on a landscape design career with commissions from neighbors and friends who appreciated his ability to design both a house and its landscape. A study trip to Italy in 1892 resulted in the publication of a monograph, *Italian Gardens*, which brought his ideas to a wider audience and attracted clients from well beyond New England.

Thus, before Charles Platt designed Roosevelt House, he was better known for his country houses, suburban estates, and gardens throughout the Northeast and as far away as Detroit, Michigan. Among his clients were art collector Charles Freer, political philosopher and journalist Herbert Croly, and steel magnate Charles G. Schwab.

Platt's New York City practice included apartment houses, office buildings, and other commercial structures. After World War I, when sons William and Geoffrey joined the firm, the range of projects expanded to include museums such as the Freer Art Gallery in Washington D.C. and the Lyme Art Gallery in Connecticut, and a redesign of Philips Academy in Andover, Massachusetts. Such large projects and extended working relationships ended with the Depression, yet, nine months before he died in September 1933, he announced the formation of the firm Charles A. Platt, William and Geoffrey Platt, indicating his faith in the future.

*On the left, Sara's gift, the double townhouse at 47–49 East 65th Street,
c. 1910, from a photo album compiled by Anna Roosevelt. (Hunter College)*

Sara's choice by showing her the new single-family Frederick Lee house by Platt on the north side of 65th Street between Park and Lexington Avenues as well as other projects by his firm.[4]

Platt's plans for the Roosevelt house were completed in June 1907 and construction began soon thereafter. It was finished a year later. The total cost of land, construction, and architect's fee was approximately $247,000.[5]

The new Roosevelt house was neo Georgian in style, constructed in buff brick with limestone trim, a style that was becoming popular on the Upper East Side for residential and cultural buildings. With its references to aristocratic English urban housing of the eighteenth and early nineteenth centuries, it was particularly appealing to families who could trace their descent to the early years of the nation's history, like the Roosevelts.[6] The family's Dutch heritage was commemorated in the shield between the third and fourth floors, bearing a cluster of roses in tribute to the family name.

The six-story Roosevelt house appeared to be one great mansion from the street, an elegant solution for the narrow property; in a lot approximately thirty-five feet wide, two visually separate units would have looked squeezed and awkward. The building had a single central entrance set behind elaborate wrought-iron doors. From the enclosed vestibule inside, steps led to a landing with two doors. Each family entered its own home, Sara to the left (or west) at No. 47, and Franklin and Eleanor to the right (or east) at No. 49. The floor plans in each unit were identical but formed a mirror image.

On the first floor of each residence, a reception room opened into a center hall with an elegant stairway curving upward along the inside wall. Past the stairway and a small hall with an elevator, service stair, and half bath, visitors entered the dining room. The

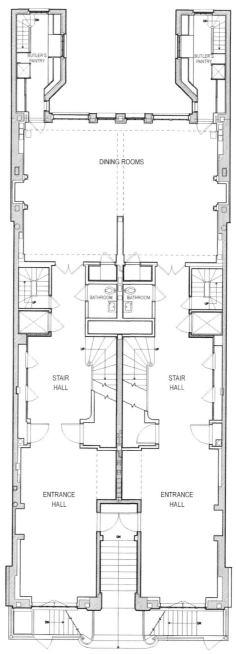

Plan of the first floor of 47–49 East 65th Street as redrawn by the architecture firm of Polshek Partnership Architects for the renovation. (Hunter College)

dining rooms in No. 47 and 49 were separated by sliding doors, making it possible to open the two spaces into one. The kitchen, pantry, and work areas, as well as a staff sitting room were in the basement, and a sub-cellar held coal and utility equipment such as the boiler. The elevators in each unit, which were often installed in the homes of the wealthy, made it possible for family and servants to live and work comfortably in what was essentially a seven-story building from the basement to the roof.

The second floor of each home had a library at the front and a drawing room at the rear, with a connecting door to the neighboring drawing room. The libraries had built in shelves and cabinets for books, and fireplaces. Eleanor later wrote in her autobiography: "The houses were narrow, but [Platt] made the most of every inch of space and built them so that the dining rooms and drawing rooms could be thrown together and made practically one big room." Such flexibility made it possible to use the adjoining rooms for social events or for the meetings of political and civic groups that Eleanor hosted in the 1920s.[7]

The third and fourth floors each had two bedrooms with baths and closet/dressing rooms. Starting on the third floor, a large innovative light court between the two residences brought light into the bathrooms as well as to the halls. Architectural historian Christopher Gray noted that "The Roosevelts surrendered usable floor area to a more civilized environment."[8]

Franklin and Eleanor's bedroom was on the third floor, and the children had rooms on the third and fourth. Connecting doors in the front rooms on the fourth floor allowed movement between houses. Servants lived and worked on the fifth and sixth floors, and an open rooftop area behind the high parapet wall facing 65th Street served as a drying roof for laundry.

The home was the Roosevelts' New York City anchor until 1941. The peripatetic lifestyle typical of wealthy families of that era took them to their homes in Hyde Park (as everyone called the family's Springwood estate) and Campobello Island for parts of the year, and Franklin's political career took them to Albany and Washington, D.C. But until Franklin became president of the United States in 1933, the family always returned to their New York home from its travels and public assignments.

In her autobiography Eleanor wrote that when she first moved into the house, she told Franklin that she "did not like to live in a house which was not in any way mine, one that I had done nothing about and which did not represent the way I wanted to live." Eleanor did acknowledge that she was at fault to some degree because she allowed her mother-in-law to make all the decisions to avoid conflict over differences, and had not developed "any individual taste or initiative."[9] She outgrew that dependency in the years to come and became an articulate and inspiring public figure herself.

When the families moved into the houses in mid-December 1908, Franklin and Eleanor had two children: Anna Eleanor, born May 3, 1906, and James, born December 23, 1907. Franklin had passed the New York bar exam, and was at the firm of Carter, Ledyard & Milburn on Wall Street.[10] Two children were born on 65th Street. Franklin Jr. was born on March 18, 1909 and died in the house, barely eight months old, on November 8, 1909. Sorrow was alleviated with joy when Elliott was born on September 23, 1910. Eleanor and Franklin also provided a home for her younger brother, Gracie Hall Roosevelt, when he was not away at school or traveling; Eleanor had looked after him since they were orphaned in 1894.

Shortly before Elliott's birth, the 1910 census recorded that Franklin, Eleanor, and their children, Anna and James, shared the house with seven employees. They were all European by birth and included the Norwegian nurse, Mari Lund; a French butler,

The young family—Franklin, Eleanor (pregnant with James), and Anna—enjoyed a summer at Campobello in 1907 before Franklin started working at the law firm of Carter, Ledyard & Milburn in New York City. (Courtesy of the Franklin D. Roosevelt Library Digital Archives)

Joseph Maillot; an Irish cook, Mary Ross; and an Irish laundress, Mary Carter. Sara had three live-in servants: Scot David Kay was the butler; his Swedish wife, Hedda Kay, was the cook; and Irish Anna Morgan, the maid.[11]

Franklin was recruited to run on the Democratic ticket in 1910 for the state senate. He won his first electoral victory in an overwhelmingly Republican area: the 26th State Senate district, comprising Putnam, Columbia, and Dutchess Counties—which included the town of Hyde Park, where the Roosevelt estate was located. He had campaigned by automobile, still a novelty at the time, which enabled him to meet a large number of voters and to give "as many as seven speeches a day delivering them from town halls, public squares, apple orchards or standing sometimes on top of haystacks," a feat that laid the foundation for his remarkable communication skills with his constituents.[12]

The family rented out the New York house and moved to Albany during the legislative session. In June 1912 they returned to 65th Street, and even though Franklin continued to serve in the legislature, the children and their caretakers stayed in New York while Eleanor commuted back and forth to Albany. Eleanor began to learn about politics, meet people from many backgrounds, and live a more independent life away from the close influence of her mother-in-law. Franklin took up the legislative agenda of the Democrats to improve conditions in factories and for women and children in the workforce. He also supported women's suffrage. During this time FDR met Louis Howe, the shrewd journalist who would mentor and advise him in his political career. Howe, Eleanor later wrote, "had made up his mind that there was a young man with a future."[13]

In March 1913, Franklin was appointed Assistant Secretary of the Navy by President Woodrow Wilson as a reward for his campaign activities on behalf of the Democratic ticket. (This allegiance caused some family discord as Theodore Roosevelt had run for a third term in 1912 as president on the Progressive ticket, having split from the Republicans.) A skilled sailor who had also practiced admiralty law, Franklin welcomed his new assignment, and the family moved to Washington, where they lived for the next seven years.

Franklin and Eleanor rented out their New York residence for part of the time to distinguished tenants, Mr. and Mrs. Thomas W. Lamont. Lamont, a graduate of Harvard College like FDR, was a well-known partner of J. P. Morgan & Company and owned the *New York Evening Post*. An expert on international finance, Lamont would be appointed by President Wilson as a representative of

Roosevelt meets with staff officers at the Philadelphia Navy Yard in October 1917, six months after the United States entered World War I. (Courtesy of the Franklin D. Roosevelt Library Digital Archives)

the U.S. Treasury on the United States Commission to the Paris Peace Conference in 1919 after World War I.

During these years, Franklin worked to build a more efficient Navy and learned about the difficult conditions and low pay of workers in the shipbuilding yards, in what Eleanor called "one of the turning points in his development."[14] When the United States entered World War I in April 1917, FDR and Eleanor became absorbed in the war effort. She spent long days working under the aegis of the Red Cross. The managerial skills she acquired and her ability to connect with people from all walks of life would prove invaluable in the years to come.

With Woodrow Wilson ailing in 1920, the Democratic Party chose a new slate for the elections: James M. Cox, the governor of Ohio, for president, and FDR for vice president. On the Republican ticket were Senator Warren G. Harding of Ohio for president, and Governor Calvin Coolidge of Massachusetts for

The Roosevelts in Washington, D.C. in 1919 during Franklin's tenure as Assistant Secretary of the Navy: (from left) Anna (1906–1975), Franklin Jr. (1914–1988), Franklin (1882–1945), Elliott (1910–1990), Eleanor (1884–1962), James (1907–1991), Sara (1854–1941), and John (1916–1981). (Courtesy of the Franklin D. Roosevelt Library Digital Archives)

vice president. The election of 1920 was the first in which women could vote for national officeholders. As a result, both political parties had well-known women speak for their candidates. Eleanor rode the campaign train with Franklin and was a visible figure at election rallies. Ironically, the Republicans drafted Eleanor's aunt (and the late Theodore Roosevelt's sister), the writer Corinne Roosevelt Robinson, to speak for them after she eloquently seconded Harding's presidential nomination at the convention. Cox and FDR were soundly defeated. FDR had lost the race, but he was now nationally known.

The Roosevelts moved back into their New York house in mid 1921, and later in the summer Eleanor and the children departed for Campobello. On August 10, shortly after he joined his family there, Franklin fell ill with polio. His legs became paralyzed and he would never walk again unassisted.

Roosevelt campaigned vigorously, but unsuccessfully, as the Democratic vice presidential candidate in 1920. Eleanor and the children can be seen center left in this photograph taken in his hometown of Hyde Park, N.Y. (Courtesy of the Franklin D. Roosevelt Library Digital Archives)

By the end of October 1921, Franklin was home at 65th Street, in the third-floor rear bedroom because, as Eleanor noted, "it was quieter there."[15] Louis Howe moved into the front third-floor bedroom where he lived weekdays to help with Franklin's business affairs and personal matters. Howe helped control press information about Franklin's condition, particularly his inability to walk, even as Franklin himself expressed optimism for a quick recovery in letters to friends.

It was an extremely difficult time for Eleanor. Although sons James and Elliott were at boarding school for much of the time, the house was crowded with the children and staff, including a nurse to help care for Franklin. Franklin Jr., who had been born August 17, 1914 at Campobello, and John Aspinwall, born March 13, 1916, in Washington D.C., and their nanny were in the fourth floor bedrooms of Sara's house, accessible through the linking doors. With no separate room left, Eleanor "slept on a bed in one of the little boys' rooms. I dressed in my husband's bathroom. In the daytime I was too busy to need a room."[16]

The strain of helping nurse Franklin as well as caring for the children, especially the teenaged Anna, were complicated by conflicts with Sara, who wanted Franklin to retire to the quieter atmosphere of Hyde Park. One day, Eleanor felt so overwhelmed that she started to sob while reading to the youngest boys. Nothing could alleviate her distress. She finally went over to Sara's house, as the elder Mrs. Roosevelt was away, found an empty room, and "locked the door and poured cold water on a towel and mopped my face. Eventually I pulled myself together."[17] The family clearly benefited from the interconnections between the two houses, and the extra space, at this time of crisis. Even during normal times the children could easily visit with their grandmother, although Eleanor later wrote of the unpredictability of Sara's visits, "You were never quite sure when she would appear, day or night."[18]

Franklin slowly began to adjust to his condition, using a wheel-chair in the house (never visibly in public) and relying on braces that locked his legs into a standing position to enable him to move with crutches or the assistance of one or two people. The elevator made it possible for him to move from floor to floor, so he could join in family life. Elliott wrote that his father designed an armless wheelchair "which was built so that it would fit in our narrow hallways and the tiny elevator."[19] The only permanent alteration to the house to accommodate Franklin's needs was the installation of extra bronze handrails in the vestibule. Portable wooden stairs

*In this unusually revealing photograph, President Roosevelt's leg braces are visible as he propels himself down the front steps of the townhouse in September 1933. (*Daily News*)*

After being paralyzed, Roosevelt found comfort in the waters in Warm Springs, Georgia. He bought land there and developed a center for people similarly afflicted. Here, the President-elect celebrates his birthday with polio-stricken children in Warm Springs in 1933. Twelve years later he would die in his cottage there. (Corbis)

with two railings fitted over the front steps outside allowed him to use his powerful arms to lift himself up and down.

Eleanor wrote that "the boys soon became entirely oblivious of the fact that their father had ever been ill. By spring he would sit on the floor with the little boys in the library, and they would play with him without the slightest idea that he was not able to do anything he wished to do in the way of rough-housing with them."[20] Franklin used the comfortable library on the second floor as an office and meeting room. He re-engaged with the activities he had taken up after leaving Washington—his responsibilities at the bonding company and, later, a new law practice as well as his work for Harvard, the Boy Scouts, and what would become the Woodrow Wilson Foundation.

Franklin's ordeal had unanticipated positive effects. Eleanor believed that dealing with his illness completed her emancipation from Sara in regard to her family's life and Joseph Lash, in his biography of the couple, concluded, "she and Franklin both emerged from the ordeal tempered, tested, and strengthened."[21] In addition, Franklin's discovery in 1924 of the beneficial effects of the waters at Warm Springs, Georgia, and his purchase of the resort in 1926 to benefit many others who had been stricken with polio, would eventually lead the Warms Springs Foundation to raise enough money through the March of Dimes campaign to fund research for a cure for polio.

In order to keep the family name current in political circles, for Franklin's sake, Eleanor became active in the Democratic Party and, for herself, engaged with civic and social causes. Her war work had awakened her, she later wrote, to "doing real work, not in being a dilettante."[22] She joined committees of the Democratic

Here, members of the Democratic Party gather in the dining room of the 65th Street house in 1924 to celebrate a successful campaign against gubernatorial candidate Theodore Roosevelt Jr. (Eleanor's first cousin), who lost to incumbent Alfred E. Smith. Eleanor and others had traveled around New York State in a car with a large steaming "teapot" mounted on the roof to remind voters of the Teapot Dome oil lease scandal under Republican President Harding. (Courtesy of the Franklin D. Roosevelt Library Digital Archives)

After meeting at a luncheon at the 65th Street house in 1924 for the leaders of women's organizations, Sara developed a close friendship with Mary McLeod Bethune. Here, the two women meet in the New York City house in December 1934. (Daily News*)*

Party (which like the Republicans had formed a separate Women's Division), the Board of the League of Women Voters, and the Women's City Club, and helped raise funds for the Women's Trade Union League. She branched out with friends Nancy Cook and Marian Dickerman, establishing Val-Kill Industries in 1925 to employ residents of the Hyde Park area in making furniture and purchasing the Todhunter School for Girls in New York City in 1926, where she taught history and literature part-time.

Eleanor frequently held gatherings at the house, taking advantage of the generous space created when the dining or drawing rooms were opened up. On one occasion in 1924, she organized a lunch for representatives of the National Council of Women and asked Sara to host. One of the attendees was Mary McLeod Bethune, president of the National Association of Colored Women. Bethune, whose parents had been slaves, was a national leader for African-American rights. She was welcomed to 65th Street by Sara and from that first meeting, Bethune remembered, "our friendship became one of the most treasured relationships of my life." In later years, Sara helped raise funds for Bethune-Cookman College in Daytona Beach, Florida, of which Bethune was the president, contributing money herself and holding fundraisers at her 65th Street house.[23]

Franklin, meanwhile, dramatically reentered public life in the summer of 1924 at the Democratic National Convention

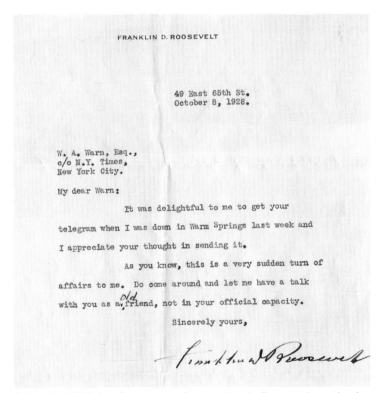

In October 1928, less than a week after accepting the Democratic nomination in the New York gubernatorial race, FDR wrote to invite his friend W.A. Warn, a New York Times *reporter, to the house on 65th Street to "have a talk" about the sudden turn of events. (Hunter College)*

at Madison Square Garden. Appearing strong and confident even while supported by his crutches, he nominated New York Governor Alfred E. Smith for president. However, corporate attorney John W. Davis secured the Democratic nomination and he, in turn, was soundly defeated by Republican candidate Calvin Coolidge for the presidency.

Four years later FDR again nominated Smith, who this time won the Democratic presidential nomination. As a result, he did not seek reelection as New York's governor. Party leaders drafted FDR to run for the position, and he campaigned with the help of Eleanor, Howe, and many others. He was elected in November 1928, defeating the Republican candidate, Attorney General Albert Ottinger, by a mere 26,000 votes out of 4.2 million cast. When Franklin took office in January 1929, the family returned to Albany, but kept the New York house open. Eleanor commuted from Albany to teach and attend meetings and spent a few days a week at 65th Street when she wasn't staying with friends. Roosevelt was reelected governor by a landslide margin of 725,000 votes for another two-year term in 1930.

Franklin's policies and the programs he initiated to help New Yorkers during the Great Depression made him an ideal candidate for president. He was elected on November 8, 1932, defeating Herbert Hoover by a popular vote of 22.8 million to 15.7 million. That day, Franklin, Eleanor, and Sara voted in Dutchess County and then motored to New York City along roads packed with cheering supporters. Franklin, Eleanor, and the three oldest children—Anna, James, and Elliott—went to the Biltmore Hotel on 42nd Street for the evening. The returns increasingly showed a Democratic victory. At about 1:40 a.m., FDR returned home where his mother greeted him at the door. "As she embraced him," the *New York Times* reported, "Mr. Roosevelt was overheard to say: 'This is the greatest night of my life.'"[24] It was at No. 49 some

The day after being elected president in November 1932, Roosevelt reads a radio address to the nation in the company of his mother; his daughter, Anna; and his oldest son, James. (AP/Worldwide)

hours later that he received a concession telegram from Hoover. On November 9, FDR spoke to the nation via NBC radio from his drawing room thanking the electorate for "this great vote of confidence and their approval of a well conceived and actively directed plan of action for economic recovery."[25]

During the next four months, until the inauguration on March 4, 1933, the house on 65th Street served as the President-elect's headquarters. Eleanor saw their home "filled with secret-service agents, and guests were scrutinized and had to be identified when Franklin was in the house."[26] Frances Perkins was invited to the house to talk with FDR about becoming the first woman to serve as Secretary of Labor. She had been Roosevelt's State Industrial Commissioner and many of the labor initiatives she fostered in New York would influence her work in the Cabinet from 1933 to 1945. On February 22, Perkins found

> the house was strangely disorderly on the ground floor. . . . It had been a nice, quiet private house where people lived, [and] it had now become a general camping place for reporters, politicians, policemen, and detectives. . . . [The entrance] hall was just piled high with overcoats, hats, umbrellas, briefcases, notebooks, sheafs of paper, red envelopes, any amount of things, not only on the chairs and tables, but on the floor. There were smoking stands, ashtrays, cigarette stubs.[27]

On March 2, 1933, the Roosevelts left No. 49 at 4:00 p.m. to travel to Washington, D.C. for FDR's inauguration as the 32nd president of the United States. His motorcar, accompanied by a large entourage, drove to lower Manhattan as enthusiastic crowds lined the streets. At Liberty Street and the Hudson River, the cars boarded a special ferry to the Jersey City terminal of the Baltimore & Ohio Railroad for the trip to the nation's capital.

The Roosevelts moved into the White House and, with his reelection to the presidency in 1936, 1940, and 1944, the family only visited No. 49 intermittently during the 1930s and 1940s. On Memorial Day weekend in 1934, when Franklin and Eleanor were in New York City to review the fleet from the deck of the heavy cruiser *Indianapolis*, they stayed at 65th Street, which was heavily guarded by police. The *New York Times* reported: "From windows of neighboring houses and of Mayfair House, directly opposite No. 49, men and women hung out in hopes of catching a

On March 2, 1933, the Roosevelts left the house on 65th Street to make their way by train to Washington for Franklin's first inauguration as president of the United States. (AP/Wide World Photos)

glimpse of the President on his return home. Private automobiles and taxicabs drove round and round the block, trying to coincide with the President's arrival, until at 5:15 the police barred traffic from the block."[28]

In January 1936 FDR made the most of another visit to New York. On the night of January 18, he spoke from the townhouse to the Trustees of the Warm Springs Foundation, who were planning the annual fundraising ball to assist polio victims in honor of the President's birthday. Their telephone conversation was broadcast over the radio.[29] The next day he and many members of the extended Roosevelt family, Democrat and Republican, traveled through a blizzard to dedicate the Theodore Roosevelt Memorial at the American Museum of Natural History. Throughout his presidency, when Franklin had a major event in the city, such as the Democratic Rally at Madison Square Garden on October 31, 1936, or other campaign activities, he stayed at the house.

When Franklin was based in Albany or Washington, various members of the family lived in the 65th Street house. Daughter Anna, her husband Curtis Dall, and their two children had to give up their house during the Great Depression and moved into the fourth floor of Sara's house in 1931. James, the oldest Roosevelt son, and his first wife, Betsey Cushing, used the house for a time in the 1930s. When Eleanor was in the city by herself, however, she often stayed at a small walk-up apartment in Greenwich Village to be near her friends and sheltered from the press. Franklin and Eleanor attempted a number of times to rent No. 49 but had no takers. Indeed, assuming they would do so, Eleanor had packed up a number of family items for the move to Washington in 1933, including a portrait of her grandfather, Theodore Roosevelt Sr. "Thinking we might rent our New York house . . . my husband had said: 'You can't rent your grandfather, take him with us.'"[30] The *New York Herald Tribune* later suggested, "no tenant was ever found. One reason was that because of the close proximity to Mrs. James Roosevelt's residence, any prospective tenant had to be acceptable to her as a neighbor."[31]

Sara Roosevelt continued to live in the house at No. 47. In 1941, Eleanor gave up her apartment in Greenwich Village to stay at No. 49 to be close to her ailing mother-in-law. They went to Hyde Park in early September and were soon joined by Franklin.

Sara died on September 7, two weeks before her 87th birthday. Added to the family's loss was the death of Eleanor's brother, Hall, several weeks later.

Sara left her New York City home to Franklin and Eleanor. They had already decided to sell the building, and a "For Sale" sign was hung outside by September 16, 1941.[32] With their children grown, Franklin and Eleanor looked forward to a post-presidential retirement that would center on the Hyde Park estate

Sara and Eleanor at Hyde Park in October 1940, a year before Sara's death at nearly 87 years of age. (Courtesy of the Franklin D. Roosevelt Library Digital Archives)

and an apartment in New York. During the following spring Eleanor spent time in New York clearing out the two houses, later recalling, "We had lived in these houses since 1908 and one can imagine the accumulation of the years. My mother-in-law never threw anything away. It was a tremendous job." By early May 1942 the houses were empty and Eleanor had moved their things into a new apartment at 29 Washington Square West.[33]

The building, put on the market for $60,000, was described as two units, each with sixteen rooms and four baths; the houses were essentially unchanged from their original state. When the nation entered World War II in December 1941, the real estate market in New York suffered, making a sale less likely.

♦

ENDNOTES

1   Linda Donn, *The Roosevelt Cousins: Growing Up Together, 1882–1924* (New York: Knopf, 2001), 95.
2   "Society at Home and Abroad," *New York Times*, March 19, 1905, X1.
3   Sara Delano Roosevelt (SDR) Diaries, Franklin Delano Roosevelt Library (FDR Library), Container 67, Diary of July 1905–December 1911. On the land purchase, see Roosevelt Family Papers, FDR Library, SDR, Container 74/75, Ledger, Entries of January 29, 1907 ($5,000) and February 25, 1907 ($74,000).
4   Deborah S. Gardner, "Charles Platt in New York City, 1900–1933," in *Shaping An American Landscape: The Art and Architecture of Charles A. Platt*, ed. by Keith N. Morgan (University of New England Press, 1995), 114–15.
5   FDR Library, Roosevelt Family Papers: SDR Container 74/75, Ledger, Payments to Charles A. Platt, 1907–08, $7,506.10, Payments to builder, James McWalters, 1907–08, $124,523.88.
6   Gardner, "Charles Platt," 114.
7   Keith N. Morgan, *Charles A. Platt: The Artist as Architect* (Cambridge, MA and New York: M.I.T. Press and The Architectural History Foundation, 1985), 137 and 138; Eleanor Roosevelt, *The Autobiography of Eleanor Roosevelt* (New York: Da Capo, 1992), 60–61.
8   Christopher Gray, "The Roosevelt Townhouse, 47–49 East 65th Street," in *Kips Bay Boys and Girls Club Decorator Show Program*, April–May 1994, 71–73.
9   Eleanor Roosevelt, *Autobiography*, 61.

10 Franklin attended Columbia Law School during the 1904–05 and 1905–06 academic years and fall 1906 but did not graduate with the class of June 1907. It was not unusual in that era to take the bar and practice law without completing the degree.

11 Thirteenth Census of the United States, 1910.

12 Mrs. James Roosevelt as told to Isabel Leighton and Gabrielle Forbush, *My Boy Franklin* (New York: Ray Long & Richard R. Smith, 1933), 74.

13 Eleanor Roosevelt, *This I Remember* (New York: Harper, 1949), 23.

14 Eleanor Roosevelt, *This I Remember*, 23.

15 Eleanor Roosevelt, *Autobiography*, 118

16 Eleanor Roosevelt, *Autobiography*, 118.

17 Eleanor Roosevelt, *Autobiography*, 119.

18 Eleanor Roosevelt, "I Remember Hyde Park: A Final Reminiscence," posthumous, *McCall's*, February 1963, 73.

19 Elliott Roosevelt and James Brough, *An Untold Story: the Roosevelts of Hyde Park* (New York: G. P. Putnam's Sons, 1973), 168.

20 Eleanor Roosevelt, *Autobiography*, 118.

21 Joseph P. Lash, *Eleanor and Franklin* (New York: Norton, 1971), 276.

22 Eleanor Roosevelt, *This Is My Story*, 347.

23 Janice Pottker, *Sara and Eleanor: The Story of Sara Delano Roosevelt and Her Daughter-in-Law, Eleanor Roosevelt* (New York: St. Martin's, 2004), 297 and 231; "Negro Drive Aided by Mrs. Roosevelt," *New York Times*, December 17, 1936, 32.

24 "Roosevelt, Buoyant, Gets Returns Here," *New York Times*, November 9, 1932, 9.

25 "President Elect Roosevelt's Radio Message To Nation on 'Victory for Liberal Thought,'" *New York Times*, November 10, 1932, 1.

26 Eleanor Roosevelt, *This I Remember*, 75.

27 Reminiscences of Frances Perkins (1951–55), Part 3, 577, in the Oral History Research Office Collection of the Columbia University Libraries, http://www.columbia.edu/cu/lweb/digital/collections/nny/perkinsf/index.html.

28 "President's Wife Stirred by Fleet," *New York Times*, June 1, 1934, 12; "Roosevelt Arrives in the City Tonight," *New York Times*, May 30, 1934, 1.

29 Geoffrey C. Ward, ed., *Closest Companion: The Unknown Story of the Intimate Friendship between Franklin Roosevelt and Margaret Suckley* (Boston: Houghton Mifflin Company, 1995), 52; "Today on the Radio," *New York Times*, January 18, 1936, 18; "President's Speech to Warm Springs Trustees," *New York Times*, January 19, 1936, 35.

30 Eleanor Roosevelt, *This I Remember*, 81; "'For Rent' Sign Hung at Roosevelt Home," *New York Times*, October 25, 1934, 1.

31 "Roosevelt Puts on the Market Town House Built by His Mother," *New York Herald Tribune*, September 16, 1941, 58.

32 "President's Home in City to Be Sold," *New York Times*, September 16, 1941, 25.

33 Eleanor Roosevelt, *Autobiography*, 235.

♦ 2 ♦

"TO LOOK UPON ALL HUMAN BEINGS WITH RESPECT": HUNTER COLLEGE CREATES A UNIQUE STUDENT CENTER AT ROOSEVELT HOUSE

The Roosevelts' double townhouse on 65th Street had been on the market for about four months when Hunter College's president, Dr. George N. Shuster, wrote to President Roosevelt on January 15, 1942.[1] Would he be interested in selling the house to the college as a center for its religious and social groups? Although Hunter had a large new building, it was pressed for space for any but instructional activities. The College, founded in 1870 to train teachers, was by 1942 a public liberal arts college with a student body of approximately 10,000 women and 350 full- and part-time faculty.

President Shuster believed that religious development contributed to the moral and ethical strength of citizens in a democracy. At the same time, he knew that a publicly supported institution needed to be sensitive to any appearance of sponsoring religious groups. Overtures from Dr. Abram L. Sachar, national director of the Hillel Foundation, led to Shuster's inquiry to the President. FDR was so taken by the idea that he lowered the purchase price from $60,000 to $50,000. Dr. Sachar embraced Shuster's proposal that the Roosevelt houses be purchased by an independent nonprofit organization created by a consortium of religious groups—Jewish, Protestant, and Catholic—who would make it available to all Hunter's students, and organized a committee to carry it forward. Joseph P. Day, prominent in New York's real estate industry, led the committee, and its honorary chairmen were Omaha banker Henry Monsky, president of the national B'nai B'rith, representing the Jewish groups; John S. Burke of the Altman Foundation (and B. Altman department store), representing the Catholic groups; and attorney Charles H. Tuttle, a former

Franklin and Eleanor Roosevelt on the day of his third inaugural as president of the United States, January 20, 1941. (Tenschert Photo Co.)

gubernatorial rival of Roosevelt's in 1930 and a member of the board of the Greater New York Federation of Churches and of the Board of Higher Education, representing Protestant groups. Businessman Aaron C. Horn served as the treasurer.

President Roosevelt wrote to Henry Monsky on March 19, 1942, "I want to do all I can to help and because I am very certain that my mother would have been greatly interested in the Interfaith House, I want to have the privilege of subscribing $1,000 in my mother's name toward the total of the $50,000 fund. I do not think, of course, that this should be publicized but I have no objection if you want to tell some of your fellow trustees about it."[2] By June 1942, the committee had raised the money to buy the house, and the sale was completed later that summer. The Hunter College Student Social, Community and Religious Clubs Association (Laws of New York, 1943, Chapter 140), with a charter to "serve without discrimination the educational, spiritual, charitable and social needs of the students of Hunter College," was signed into law by Governor Thomas E. Dewey on March 20, 1943.

Eleanor Roosevelt was the guest speaker at the Hunter College commencement on June 24, 1942 when Aaron Horn announced that a "committee of thirty-three citizens" would give the Roosevelt property as a gift to Hunter College for use as a community house. The Sara Delano Roosevelt Interfaith House would be dedicated, noted Horn, to "the ideal of religious freedom and the democratic way of living." President Shuster replied, in accepting the gift, that FDR considered its new use as "the finest memorial to [his] mother." He also reported that the building would serve as a meeting place for 120 extracurricular organizations that expressed the students' cultural, political, religious, and academic interests. Characterizing Hunter as the "largest college for women in the world," Shuster predicted that the religious and civic activities at the Roosevelt House would "prepare college girls

A group of students, reflective of Hunter College's long history of integration, uses the library at 47 East 65th Street in the 1950s. Artist Frank Salisbury's portrait of FDR can be seen over the fireplace. (Hunter College)

in the best possible way for the 'new functions of leadership which will unquestionably be open to women when the war is over.'"[3]

The architecture firm of Shreve, Lamb & Harmon converted the residences into a public building. The firm had previously designed the Empire State Building (1931) as well as the college's new building at 695 Park Avenue. The general layout of the 65th Street building was kept intact but walls were removed almost completely between the dining and drawing rooms to create large common spaces for meetings, academic forums, and social events. The family's old stoves were removed and added to the scrap metal drive conducted by the college (along with the rest of the city) to salvage metal for war munitions.[4]

The Roosevelt House League (later the Association of Neighbors and Friends of Hunter College House) raised funds to furnish and decorate the center. The committee included Doris Shuster, wife of Hunter's president; Blanche Horn and Hélène Tuttle, wives of the fundraisers; and Ruth O'Day Ridder and Evelyn Feil Picker. Mrs. Ridder and her husband, Victor, were prominent in Catholic circles, and his family was active in German-American affairs in New York City. Victor had taken the family's ownership of *The New Yorker Staats Zeitung und Herold* to new heights, building a national newspaper chain (eventually Ridder-Knight). In September 1935 FDR appointed Ridder as the federal administrator of the New York City Works Progress Administration (WPA), the largest unit of FDR's important New Deal program serving more unemployed people than any other in the nation.

Self Portrait by Francesco di Cristofano (c. 1516), donated by the Kress Foundation, was one of the significant works of art that found a new home at Roosevelt House. (Hunter College)

As plans for the interior of the House coalesced, the Alumnae Association, Hunter professors, and student groups secured furnishings and funds, while interior decorators from leading department stores—B. Altman & Co., Bloomingdales, and W. & J. Sloan—advised. Among the most involved alumnae was Ruth Lewinson, class of 1916, an attorney who had organized legal-aid assistance for service families. A former trustee of Hunter College and member of the Board of Higher Education, she would become president of the Alumnae Association in 1945.

Donations from Hunter alumnae and others filled the rooms with furniture, curtains, rugs, and artwork. Among the paintings given to the House was the sixteenth-century *Self Portrait* by Francesco di Cristofano (c. 1516), donated by the Kress Foundation as part of a major initiative to place outstanding art in museums and colleges around the country.[5] James Picker and his wife, Evelyn Feil Picker, a 1905 graduate of Hunter and a former schoolteacher, paid for the furnishings in the combined drawing rooms on the second floor. The space became known as the "Picker Room" and was used for "small dances, receptions, and meetings of a general nature."[6] A Russian immigrant who had come to the United States in 1900, Picker manufactured and distributed X-ray equipment. The wartime sales of Picker's mobile field X-ray unit were so great that he returned $4 million to the U.S. government in gratitude for the opportunities the country had given him.

Professor Joseph Cummings Chase, former head of the Hunter College art department, painted four portraits for the house of Hunter students in the service of their country.[7] A skilled artist, he had been sent by the government to Europe during World War I to draw American generals and soldiers and carried out similar commissions in New York during World War II. In addition, Chase had painted portraits of Theodore Roosevelt, Woodrow Wilson, Warren G. Harding, and Franklin Roosevelt.

President Roosevelt contributed money, books, and mementos for the establishment of a library in No. 49 in memory of his mother. A portrait of Sara Roosevelt, a copy of the 1940 original at Hyde Park by the artist Douglas Granville Chandor, was hung in the room. The second library, at No. 47, featured a portrait of President Roosevelt, a copy from the original at the Metropolitan Museum of Art by the accomplished English painter Frank Salisbury. When renovations were finished in November 1943, Dr. Shuster told the *Alumnae News* that more than 1,000 people from across the United States had contributed money to the project. It was the first of its kind in the city, he noted, because of its commitment to "promoting inter-faith activity and fraternalism among the different religions."[8]

The Dedication of the Sara Delano Roosevelt Interfaith Memorial House

The dedication ceremony took place on November 22, 1943 in the Hunter College auditorium, two years after Sara's death. Eleanor Roosevelt represented the family as her husband was in Cairo, Egypt, meeting with British Prime Minister Winston Churchill and General Chiang Kai-shek of China. Mayor Fiorello LaGuardia, Charles Tuttle, Henry Monsky, Dr. William Agar, and other friends of the college participated in the ceremony. Clergy from Protestant, Catholic, and Jewish groups provided an invocation, readings, and a benediction. The city's radio station, WNYC, broadcast the proceedings.

The distinguished speakers focused on the important role the Interfaith House would have in the lives of Hunter students, building not only cooperation among different religions, but also among different races. In the midst of World War II, such support for interfaith and interracial cooperation served as a counterpoint to the ideology of hate promoted by Nazi Germany.

When Roosevelt House was dedicated as part of Hunter College in November 1943, Franklin Roosevelt was in Cairo meeting with Chiang Kai-shek and Winston Churchill. He went on to meet with Joseph Stalin (left) and Churchill (right) in Tehran. (Library of Congress Prints and Photographs Division)

The performers featured in the dedication ceremony supported the mission of the Interfaith House and the diversity of the college community. Anne Roselle, a Hungarian-born soprano with the Metropolitan Opera, offered an aria from *Aida* on the grief of exile from a conquered homeland, a fitting wartime theme for the many refugees and daughters of refugees in the Hunter community. Aubrey Pankey, an internationally known, classically trained African-American baritone, filled the hall "with effortless ease" as he sang a Negro spiritual. His presence underscored Hunter's commitment to its interracial student body.

Eleanor Roosevelt, introduced by President Shuster, relayed FDR's congratulatory message, which described the House as "the finest memorial" to his mother, and read from a letter he had written:

> I feel that my dear Mother would be very happy in the realization of plans whereby the old home in East Sixty-fifth Street, with all of its memories of joy and sorrow, is now to become Interfaith House, dedicated to mutual understanding and good will among students matriculating in Hunter College.
>
> It is to me of happy significance that this place of sacred memories is to become the first college center established for the high purpose of mutual understanding among Protestant, Jewish, and Catholic students. I hope this movement for toleration will grow and prosper until there is a similar establishment in every institution of higher learning in the land, the spirit of which shall be unity in essentials; liberty in non-essentials; and in all things, charity.[9]

Eleanor's own remarks about Sara were similar to those published in her national column, "My Day" in New York's *World-Telegram* two days later:

> My mother-in-law had traveled a great deal all of her life, beginning with her trip to China when she was a very small child, so she had a liking for many different countries and their people. Though she had been brought up as a Unitarian and became an Episcopalian after her marriage, she was very tolerant of all other religions. I think she would have been interested in having work go on in these houses which will bring about greater understanding and tolerance in young people.[10]

Eleanor reiterated, "No houses could have a better background for the use they will now serve. Always in both houses there was an effort to look on all human beings with respect, and to have a true understanding of the points of view of others." For Eleanor, the Interfaith House would "carry on the ideals and spirit of Sara Delano Roosevelt."[11] This spirit was evident not only in the

Roosevelts' interests in interfaith cooperation, but also in their efforts on behalf of African Americans in their private and public lives. Sara's friendship with Mary McLeod Bethune, which began in 1924, was but one example.

Eleanor, too, was publicly engaged in upholding the rights of African Americans. She had resigned her membership in the Daughters of the American Revolution in 1939 when the organization refused to allow the great African-American contralto Marian Anderson to perform in its concert hall because of her race. The First Lady had then arranged for Anderson to sing on Easter Sunday at the Lincoln Memorial in Washington, D.C.,

Three months after Eleanor arranged a concert at the Lincoln Memorial for singer Marian Anderson, she presented the NAACP's Spingarn Medal for outstanding achievement by an African American to Anderson in Philadelphia. (University of Pennsylvania, Rare Book and Manuscript Library, Marian Anderson Collection)

in April 1939. Soon after, Franklin and Eleanor invited her to perform at the White House at a state dinner in June 1939 for King George IV and Queen Elizabeth.[12]

As the dedication ceremony for Roosevelt House continued, Dr. William Agar, a founder and then acting president of Freedom House, a consortium that upheld the fight for freedom and democracy against the totalitarian forces then ravaging Europe and Asia, focused his speech on interracial amity. He emphasized that cooperation among races was as important as interfaith cooperation and that peace was dependent on all nations treating all their citizens equally.[13] Mayor LaGuardia asserted that progress had been made in the city toward "inter-faith and inter-racial understanding" which would be the means of "conquering hatred, prejudice and ignorance."[14]

The last speaker, Dr. Frank Kingdon, chairman of the International Rescue and Relief Committee, asked his audience to go beyond tolerance to make a real change in their own lives and the lives of all they met. His views were echoed in the *Hunter Bulletin* in an editorial published a week after the dedication, supporting the mission and values of the interfaith program, a first in the United States:

> The Sara Delano Roosevelt Memorial House was not dedicated as a 'house of toleration,' nor shall we allow it to become one. It is not enough for each of us to tolerate the religions different from the one we believe in; it is not enough if we become just passive by-standers in this new religious venture. For we shall not be serving the full purpose of the House unless we all learn, recognize, understand, and appreciate the fundamental similarities and differences of the three faiths.[15]

Eleanor visited Roosevelt House a week after the dedication ceremony. She wrote in her "My Day" column that she found it filled with students in all the rooms and admired how it had been adapted for its new uses. She was "sure that this is going to be a successful and useful experiment [in] the willingness of young people of different religious faiths to live and work under the same roof."[16] Her hopes would be fulfilled.

Roosevelt House was filled with activities for almost half a century. Student groups drew lots for their office assignments in Roosevelt House. The religious groups had their offices in No. 49—the Hillel Foundation on the third floor, the Newman Club on the fourth, and the Protestant groups on the fifth. No. 47 was home to social and athletic groups: the Athletic Association, Pan-Hellenic Association (the 18 Greek-letter sororities), and the Alumnae Association, as well as the social groups known as "House Plans." The Toussaint L'Ouverture Society for the Study of African-American History and Culture, founded in 1936, also

A club meets in Roosevelt House in the 1950s. (Hunter College)

opened an office there. The college had a seventy-year commitment to the education of African Americans, having admitted
black students in 1873, three years after it opened its doors. In
1944, in response to a campaign by the Toussaint L'Ouverture
Society, Hunter introduced a course called "Negro History and
Culture," taught by Adelaide M. Cromwell, the first African-
American woman appointed to Hunter's faculty.[17]

The building was open long hours to meet the needs of the
students. Organizations in residence as well as other student and
alumnae groups and academic departments had meetings, lec-
tures, and special events in the common areas. There was a live-in
custodian and a social manager for the house. Four to five hundred

*During World War II, students held canteen evenings for soldiers and sailors temporar-
ily based in New York. (Hunter College)*

students might use the building during an evening. Hunter students also held weddings in the building, in part because of its modest rental fee of $50.[18]

A 1947 graduate, Elizabeth Thal Kahn, married in Roosevelt House. In 1937 her family had reached the United States as refugees; a decade later she completed her studies at Hunter and got married at Roosevelt House. She recalls:

> This was such a wonderful privilege for me since I always associated President Roosevelt with our escape from Germany and our well being in this country. To be married under the portrait of Sara Delano Roosevelt who looked sternly upon us as if saying 'This is a serious matter' was awesome. . . . Neither my husband nor I could have ever accomplished the things we did in our lives without the [free] City colleges.[19]

Activities at the House changed with the times. During World War II students held weekly canteen evenings for soldiers and sailors who were based temporarily in New York. Ruth Goodman Cohen, a 1946 graduate, remembered:

> It was considered our patriotic duty to attend the Roosevelt House canteen to try to build the morale of these fellows. Dancing with a partner wearing paratrooper boots was hard on one's feet! These battle-bound young men were able to forget briefly what lay ahead, by chatting and relaxing in the pleasant surroundings of Roosevelt House's upstairs salon [former drawing rooms]. The House represented for me a bright spot in a terrifying world of depressing events. . . . It was an oasis of stability in a hideously violent world.[20]

For many Hunter students who came from poor, working-class families, Roosevelt House was a beautiful and luxurious place to visit and enjoy college activities. Antoinette Passarello, a 1970 graduate, recalled her first visit to Roosevelt House: "Since I had come from a large, blue-collar family in Queens, my world opened when I attended Hunter College. I was thrilled to be able to actually enter one of the magnificent brownstones [Roosevelt House] near the college." Like New York City itself, Hunter College was a melting pot for all ethnic, racial, and religious groups. The vision of the first handbook about Roosevelt House had been fulfilled: "We believe that what is called 'intercultural education' is not something to be found in a textbook but rather to be derived from the experience of living."[21]

From time to time, the House also hosted special public events. As the tenth anniversary of the opening of Roosevelt House in 1953 coincided with New York City's 300th anniversary as an incorporated city, the Association of Neighbors and Friends of Roosevelt House sponsored a salute to the "Dutch Founders of Our City"

Artist and Hunter faculty member Joseph Cummings Chase painted portraits of four Hunter students serving their country, to be installed in Roosevelt House. Doris Coles, class of 1941, served in the WAVES. Her portrait was initially placed in the second floor reception room. (Hunter College)

with an exhibition of eighty-four Dutch paintings and etchings at the House. The art included fifty seventeenth-century works on loan from the University of Leyden in the Netherlands. As the Roosevelt family had come to America from the Netherlands in the 1640s, this exhibition was of particular significance.[22]

In 1960, the House entered Hollywood lore when scenes for the movie *Sunrise at Campobello*, starring Ralph Bellamy as FDR and Greer Garson as Eleanor, were filmed there. Based on the successful 1958 play by Dore Schary, the story takes up FDR's life from the time he was stricken with polio in 1921 to his political comeback at the 1924 Democratic Convention.[23]

Sixty-five years after it was built, the former home of Franklin, Eleanor, and Sara Roosevelt was designated a New York City Landmark in 1973 and then was placed on the National Register of Historic Places in 1980. However, in 1992, Roosevelt House was closed, in serious need of renovation, and Hunter College began to seek a way to return it to its former glory as a vital part of the college community. This was achieved following a major renovation and Roosevelt House reopened during the 2009–2010 academic year as a Public Policy Institute with room for teaching, research, and public programs.

ENDNOTES

1 Original correspondence at the FDR Library, President's Personal File (PPF), 1-H, Special Folder. Copies in the Hunter College Archives. For an excellent discussion of the Roosevelts relationship with Hunter College, see Jeffrey A. Kroessler, "Eleanor Roosevelt and Hunter College," presented at the conference, "The Vision of Eleanor Roosevelt: World Citizen Ahead of Her Time," at Hofstra University, September 30–October 2, 1999.
2 FDR to Henry Monsky, March 19, 1942, Roosevelt House Collection, Hunter College Archives.
3 "Homes of the President and Mother to Be Hunter Community House," *New York Times*, June 25, 1942, 1, 18; "President 'Happy' Over Hunter Deal," *New York Times*, June 26, 1942, 23.
4 "Manhattan Drive for Scrap Metal Opened," *New York Times*, October 14, 1942, 18.

5   Hunter Archives, Box 1, F11, "The Sara Delano Roosevelt Memorial House, November 1943" and George Shuster to Samuel H. Kress, October 22, 1943; The Kress Foundations, http://www.kressfoundation.org.
6   "Roosevelt Home to be Dedicated," *New York Times*, October 17, 1943, 50. Information about the Pickers' involvement from retired State court judge Dorothea E. Donaldson, class of 1931, letter to Danielle Cylich, July 30, 2001. See also "James Picker, X-Ray Pioneer and Founder of Company, Dies," *New York Times*, May 30, 1963, 12, and "Mrs. James Picker, Donor to Colleges," *New York Times*, January 18, 1968, 39.
7   Hunter Archives, Box 1, F11. Three WAVES and one WAC. Joseph Cummings Chase note.
8   Quote, typescript, George Shuster address on dedication, November 22, 1945. Hunter College Archives, B8, F1. Letters FDR and Shuster, September 14 and 16, 1942; "Sara Delano Roosevelt House in New Togs," *Alumnae News*, November 1943, 1–2; press release, "Former Presidential Conference Room, Now a Library," *New York Times*, November 18, 1943, 19. Ruth Lewinson to and from Myron C. Taylor, May 7, 1943 and June 2, 1943 re Salisbury painting, Shuster to Taylor, June 7, 1943.
9   *Hunter Bulletin*, November 16 and 30, 1943; President's letter to Richard E. Bishop, November 4, 1943 (PPF file), *Alumnae News*, December 1943, 1; "President Pleased by Home's New Use," *New York Times*, November 15, 1943, 27.
10 *Alumnae News*, December 1943, 3; *Hunter Bulletin*, November 30, 1943; "The First Lady Speaks at Dedication Here," *New York Times*, November 23, 1943, 27. "My Day," November 24, 1943, in the Eleanor Roosevelt Papers Project at The George Washington University, http://www.gwu.edu/~erpapers/myday/.
11 "The First Lady Speaks at Dedication Here," *New York Times*, November 23, 1943, 27; *Hunter Bulletin*, November 30, 1943.
12 "King Will Hear Songs of Our Land," *New York Times*, May 23, 1939, 14.
13 *Alumnae News*, December 1943, 2.
14 *Alumnae News*, December 1943, 2; *Hunter College Bulletin*, November 30, 1943; "The First Lady Speaks at Dedication Here," *New York Times*, November 23, 1943, 27.
15 "The Sara Delano Roosevelt Memorial House," *Hunter Bulletin*, November 30, 1943.
16 "My Day," December 1, 1943, Eleanor Roosevelt Papers Project, GWU, http://www.gwu.edu/~erpapers/myday/.
17 The Toussaint L'Ouverture Society succeeded an interracial sorority that Hunter faculty had helped organize. See George N. Shuster, "An Autobiography," in *On the Side of Truth: George N. Shuster, an Evaluation with Readings*, ed. by Vincent P. Lannie (South Bend, IN: University of Notre Dame Press, 1974), 25.
18 Thomas E. Blantz, *George N. Shuster: On the Side of Truth* (Notre Dame, IN: University of Notre Dame Press, 1993), 147. On African-American students and Cromwell at Hunter, see Linda M. Perkins, "African-American Women and Hunter College: 1873–1945," *The ECHO, Journal of the Hunter College Archives*, (1995): 22–23.
19 Elizabeth Thal Kahn to Danielle Cylich, Hunter College, c. summer 2001.
20 Ruth Goodman Cohen to Danielle Cylich, Hunter College, July 21, 2001.
21 Antoinette Passarello to Danielle Cylich, Hunter College, July 22, 2001; Handbook, *The Sara Delano Roosevelt House*, December 1945.
22 "Art Exhibition Opens at Roosevelt House," *New York Times*, April 29. 1953, 17.
23 On the play, and Schary's research and consultation with the Roosevelt family, see Dore Schary, "Dramatizing a Thirty-four Month Ordeal in F.D.R.'s Life," *New York Times*, January 26, 1958, X1, 3.

◆ 3 ◆

AN ENDURING FRIENDSHIP:
THE ROOSEVELTS AND
HUNTER COLLEGE

Well before the dedication of Sara Delano Roosevelt Memorial House in 1943, Franklin and Eleanor were aware of Hunter College, just three blocks from their New York City home.

Franklin Roosevelt's only official visit to the Manhattan campus of Hunter College was on October 28, 1940. Campaigning for his third term as president, Roosevelt traveled in a motorcade around the city with Mayor Fiorello LaGuardia and other Democratic politicians. They visited all five boroughs to attend ground-breaking ceremonies and view government-funded projects. One of those projects was Hunter College's new Park Avenue building.[1]

The college's 1873 Gothic-style building had been destroyed by fire on February 14, 1936, and Mayor LaGuardia had secured $6.5 million from the Public Works Administration, one of Roosevelt's key New Deal programs to rebuild the economy, to replace the old structure with a much larger building. The firm of Shreve, Lamb & Harmon designed a spare, modern-style

FDR spoke in Hunter's Assembly Hall on October 28, 1940 to celebrate the opening of the college's new building, funded in part by his Public Works Administration. (Corbis)

sixteen-story building with classrooms, labs, a cafeteria, a swimming pool, broadcasting studios, a small theater (later known as the Sylvia and Danny Kaye Playhouse), a 2,600-seat Assembly Hall (one of the largest in the city), and a 600-student elementary school. When the building was dedicated on October 8, 1940, Mayor LaGuardia defied opponents of the federal pump-priming program "to criticize this expenditure. It is," he asserted, "one of America's best investments."[2]

The President's visit later that month prompted a "final dedication."[3] Aided by his son James, FDR was accompanied on the stage by Mayor LaGuardia, President Shuster, Governor Herbert Lehman, and Dr. Ordway Tead, chairman of the Board of Higher Education. Some thirty years later, student Anna M. Trinsey recalled the extraordinary sound of "all 2,600 of us expressing our hearts' welcome."[4] Freshman Marian Shomer Greene remembered the moment too:

> His appearance proved more moving than anyone anticipated, because we hadn't known how crippled he was. . . . A lump rose in my throat at the sight of the effort our President had to make to walk just eight steps. I glanced

Franklin Delano Roosevelt and Hunter College

October 28, 1940: Franklin Roosevelt visits Hunter's Manhattan campus to attend the final dedication of new Park Avenue building during campaign visit to New York City. Speaks in Assembly Hall.

Spring–Summer 1942: Franklin and Eleanor Roosevelt sell Roosevelt House to Hunter College Student Social, Community and Religious Club Association.

June 24, 1942: Gift of Roosevelt House is announced at college graduation ceremony.

March 20, 1943: Governor Thomas E. Dewey signs incorporation charter for Sara Delano Roosevelt Memorial House.

October 21, 1944: FDR visits Hunter's Bronx campus, as part of campaign trip, to review WAVES training center.

January 30, 1972: Commemoration of 90th anniversary of FDR's birth.

around at the audience, and many people had tears in their eyes. It was now clear why Roosevelt so often had James at his side. When he reached the podium, he stood by himself, holding on to the desk. We applauded him wildly, while he smiled the famous Roosevelt smile.[5]

When the audience quieted, the President commented "his New York home was only two blocks from Hunter and that he . . . had known that it needed a new building." He urged students to train as teachers, for "in many parts of the country we still have the problem of providing better qualified teachers, to bring the younger generation to maturity so that they will have a better chance in this complicated civilization." Mayor LaGuardia, Roosevelt told the audience, "comes to Washington and tells me a sad story. The tears run down my cheeks and tears run down his cheeks and the first thing I know he has wangled another $50,000,000." Roosevelt concluded on a more serious note, asking the students to keep alive the "patriotism, love of our nation, that

Mayor Fiorello LaGuardia, pictured here with Eleanor Roosevelt in 1934, was instrumental in bringing New Deal programs to New York City, including the funds from the Public Works Administration to construct a new building for Hunter College. (Courtesy of the Franklin D. Roosevelt Library Digital Archives)

began many, many generations ago, and that is still with us, as we know, in this great city."[6]

Franklin would visit Hunter only one more time because of the heavy burden of the war. He went to Hunter's Bronx campus during a campaign trip in October 1944 to review the WAVES (Women Accepted for Voluntary Emergency Service. The campus had been taken over by the government to create the largest training center in the United States for this branch of the Navy, which had been established in July 1942.

Some months before the President's visit to Hunter College in 1940, Eleanor Roosevelt had already begun her association with Hunter, both formally and informally. She would continue to be engaged with the college until the year before her death in 1962.

Mrs. Roosevelt's first visits to Hunter in 1940 brought her to the offices of the *Echo*, the college's magazine, to talk with the staff writers. She continued to drop in about once a month during the next year, without advance notice or bodyguards. She chatted with the students, listened to popular music with them, and read the articles they wrote. Marion Shomer Greene marveled at how nonchalant her parents were about the First Lady's visits with their daughter: "My father, too, appeared to take the First Lady's visits in stride. His parents had been immigrants who came here expecting freedom and equality, and the fact that the President's wife was conversing with his teenage daughter struck him as entirely appropriate."[7] Eleanor met with students at the college and at other events. She even invited one student, Naomi Block (Hunter, 1942), a student leader, to visit the White House where she met the President, the Vice President, and Winston Churchill.[8]

Eleanor's dedication to education, the evolving role of women in the United States, and the development of engaged citizens led her to make more than two dozen visits to Hunter College over the next twenty years. She spoke at and attended events sponsored by the Hunter College community and by other organizations invested in the social, economic, and political causes she supported as First Lady and as chair of the Commission on Human Rights of the United Nations' Economic and Social Council. As President Shuster later wrote, "the warm spirit of Eleanor Roosevelt hovered over the campus during all the years I was there. She came again and again and again, asking no emolument whatever, always attracting everybody who could get into the hall."[9] George Shuster and Eleanor Roosevelt were friends and believed in many of the same causes. Shuster also stayed in touch with President Roosevelt, who asked him for help in placing American and foreign scholars in the United States, particularly during the war.

The themes Eleanor Roosevelt addressed in her official visits to Hunter College in 1941 and in 1942 as the U.S. entered World War II exemplified her concerns as First Lady. She spoke to the women of Hunter College on "Education in a Democracy," "The Benefits of Extending Free Higher Education," "Can College Students Continue in Wartime?" and "What Contributions Women Can Make During the War and in the Post-War Reconstruction Period." Eleanor, as assistant director of the federal Office of Civilian Defense, also spoke at the 1941 conference of the New York Women's Trade Union League at Hunter College.

Mrs. Roosevelt first visited Hunter officially on February 19, 1941 as the second speaker in a series entitled "Education in a Democracy."[10] She addressed the meaning of democracy in the lives of students, stressing that the freedoms of democracy required "responsibility, discipline, and participation." She impressed her listeners by speaking "in a ringing voice without a note, without a moment's hesitation, without even the change of a word." In a question-and-answer session, she defended the Lend-Lease bill; avowed that peace groups should be given public forums; and confirmed her support for proposed federal anti-lynching

Eleanor first spoke to the Hunter College community in February 1941, addressing students on "Education and Democracy." She was introduced by Dr. George N. Shuster, president of the college, who became a good friend and colleague. (Corbis)

legislation. The need for improved race relations was highlighted by a question from an audience member: "Can and will the Negro continue to be loyal in the face of discrimination?" Her answer was brief and definitive: "I have never known a case where any Negro citizen of the country showed a lack of loyalty."[11] President Roosevelt's Executive Order 8802 of June 25, 1941 gave legal weight to this view that he and Eleanor shared. His order, the first presidential directive on race since Reconstruction, declared, "There shall be no discrimination in the employment of workers in defense industries and in Government, because of race, creed, color, or national origin."[12]

THE WHITE HOUSE
WASHINGTON

January 14, 1942

Mr. Joseph Curran, President
National Maritime Union
346 West 17th Street
New York, N. Y.

My dear Mr. Curran:

I am informed that the discrimination against colored
seamen, referred to in your telegram of January 2nd, was elimi-
nated by the action of the United States Maritime Commission on
the day it occurred.

It is the policy of the Government of the United States to
encourage full participation in the National Defense program by
all citizens, regardless of race, creed, color, or national origin,
in the firm belief that the democratic way of life within the
nation can be defended successfully only with the help and support
of all groups within its borders.

The policy was stated in my Executive Order signed on June
25, 1941. The order instructed all parties making contracts with
the Government of the United States to include in all defense contracts thereafter a provision obligating the contractor not to dis-
criminate against any worker because of race, creed, color or
national origin.

Questions of race, creed and color have no place in deter-
mining who are to man our ships. The sole qualifications for a
worker in the maritime industry, as well as in any other industry,
should be his loyalty and his professional or technical ability
and training.

Sincerely yours,

Franklin D. Roosevelt

*The mobilization of men and women for the war effort inevitably brought racial issues
to the fore. In this letter to Joseph Curran of the National Maritime Union, FDR
signals his disapproval of discrimination against blacks in all branches of the service,
including the merchant marine, and cites his executive order of June 25, 1941. (Gilder
Lehrman Collection)*

Perhaps the most difficult question Eleanor faced during this visit was whether the United States would enter the war. After acknowledging her own opposition to war, Mrs. Roosevelt supported providing Great Britain with the assistance it needed to win against Germany and concluded, "there are some things that one would rather die than see happen. I haven't faced that question yet, but will face it if I have to—and so will you." To a writer from the *Alumnae News*, she had shown herself "not only as the First Lady of the Land but also as an honest, fearless, clear-thinking woman who has the courage and the integrity to be whole-heartedly herself."[13]

Mrs. Roosevelt also took time that day to sit down for an interview with a small group of students, arranged by the *Echo*, where the conversation focused on the changing role of women in public life in the decades after suffrage. Eleanor predicted that "as women come out of the home and into the community they are going to be considered more as men have been considered in the past—as part of the community."[14]

Mrs. Roosevelt returned to Hunter on June 24, 1942 for commencement to hear the announcement about Roosevelt House and to address the graduates. By then, the United States was at war, so she spoke about the responsibilities women had in their communities and the nation. She urged them to understand the objectives for which the United States and the United Nations were fighting: "Freedom to worship God in our own way; freedom to have the kind of government we desire to live under anywhere in the world; freedom from want . . . and freedom from racial discrimination." She concluded, "You don't build that kind of freedom without working for it everyday."[15]

Eleanor wrote about this event in her daily newspaper column, "My Day": "It was amazing to see so many young women

(Text continues on page 80.)

1941 • **February 19**: Speaks on "Education and Democracy."

• **October 25**: Speaks at New York Women's Trade Union League conference.

• **November 25**: Speaks on "The Benefits of Extending Free Higher Education."

1942 • **June 24**: Gives main address at 82nd commencement of Hunter College. Gift of Roosevelt House is announced.

• **August 12**: Speaks on "What Contributions Women Can Make During the War and in the Post-War Reconstruction Period."

• **December 5–6**: Participates in roundtable on "Can College Students Continue in Wartime?" at joint conference of Hunter College War Committee and International Student Service.

1943 • **August 2**: Speaks at review of WAVES at the Bronx campus.

• **November 22**: Speaks at Roosevelt House dedication.

• **November 29**: First visit to refurbished Roosevelt House.

1945 • **October 4**: Speaks at memorial ceremony sponsored by the Netherlands-Jewish Society.

1946 • **February 26**: Speaks at District Cancer Forum sponsored by Roosevelt House League.

• **February 28**: Speaks at forum sponsored by Union for Democratic Action on the importance of the United Nations.

• **April 29**: Elected chair of the Commission on Human Rights of the Economic and Social Council at organizational meetings of United Nations at Bronx campus of Hunter College.

• **May 29**: Speaks on "The World We Have and the World We Want" at American Jewish Congress national convention.

• **July 14**: Speaks at Annual Bastille Day celebration sponsored by France Forever.

1948 • **January 16**: Speaks at memorial to honor FDR held by Bronx Committee of Associate Alumnae of Hunter College.

1949 • **November 15**: Speaks on "The Human Rights Document in Relation to Family Life" at Tri-State Council on Family Relations.

1950 • **April 25**: Speaks at Roosevelt House League program.

• **October 1**: Receives First Annual Cooperation Award for aid to cooperative movement at Cooperative Enterprises Founders Day celebration.

- **c. October 17**: Speaks on "The United Nations and the World Today" at O.R.T. Federation, Women's American 11th biennial convention.

1951 • **October 19**: Speaks on importance of discussing controversial issues "despite efforts that have been made in various parts of the country to impose conformity of thought" at New York State Teachers Association, South Eastern Zone, 106th annual meeting.

1953 • **April 23**: Speaks at and is honored by Metropolitan New York Council of the American Associations for the United Nations.
- **April 29**: Speaks on "Meeting Youth Around the World" at 10th anniversary of Roosevelt House.

1954 • **October 20**: Attends reception sponsored by the American Association for the United Nations and the Association of Neighbors and Friends of Hunter College for United Nations Week.

1955 • **May 20**: Speaks on "The United Nations and the Far East."

1958 • **March 18**: Speaks on "When Roosevelt House Was a Roosevelt Home" at 15th anniversary of Roosevelt House opening.

1960 • **January 25**: Attends Hunter Convocation honoring President Shuster on his retirement.
- **February 13**: Speaks on "The Changing World and the Responsibility of Education" at the 90th birthday of Hunter College celebration at Alumni Association lunch at Astor Hotel.
- **March 18**: Speaks at memorial service for Mrs. Adele Rosenwald Levy sponsored by Citizens Committee for Children of New York, Inc.

1961 • **October 2**: Eleanor Roosevelt and Senator Jacob Javits speak at Hunter about the Peace Corps.

* * * * *

1974 • **October 10**: 90th anniversary program of Eleanor Roosevelt's birth.

1982 • **December 1982**: Eleanor Roosevelt featured at First Lady Conference.

graduating, almost a thousand girls took their degrees. It was an inspiring evening and I shall watch with interest the girls whom I have had the pleasure of meeting in this class as they grow into their new responsibilities."[16] Eleanor's visits to Hunter during the war years were especially valued because she had so many other responsibilities, including travel assignments from the President to far-flung war zones. She empathized with the concerns of the Hunter students and their families because her four sons were all on active duty, often in dangerous assignments: FDR Jr. and John were in the Navy, James was in the Marines, and Elliott was in the Army Air Forces.

Eleanor's "My Day" column often mentioned Hunter students who obviously felt free to approach her, an unprecedented accessibility for a first lady. In May 1942, for example, several students met her at a gathering downtown where Eleanor was on the program to discuss Axis propaganda. They walked with her to her apartment afterwards. She wrote, "They are tremendously proud of the way in which Hunter College has met every war demand. . . . Dr. George Shuster . . . has the gift of inspiring the students to take seriously their responsibilities to the community."[17]

Eleanor frequently mentioned Hunter as an exemplar, whether it was a war drive for metals, or educating women about issues they might encounter in war or after their discharge from military service. "I am sure the college will do its part, for one always finds Hunter thinking ahead on the problems of the day where girls are concerned."[18]

After the war, President Harry S. Truman appointed Eleanor to the U.S. delegation to the United Nations (1945–1953). At a meeting at Hunter sponsored by the Union for Democratic Action in February 1946, she characterized the U.N. as "the alternative to [world] chaos," and went on to say of American leadership: "The success of the United Nations Organization is of desperate

Eleanor, in a Red Cross uniform as she was representing that agency, stopped on Guadalcanal during a six-week tour of U.S. outposts in the Pacific in 1943. Her work with the Red Cross during World War I had been vital to her emergence in the public arena, and in World War II she continued her activities at home and abroad. (Hunter College)

Eleanor Roosevelt was elected chair of the Commission on Human Rights at the organizing meetings of the United Nations. The international organization was then meeting at its interim headquarters on the Bronx campus of Hunter College in April 1946. The commission produced the Universal Declaration of Human Rights which was adopted by the U.N. in December 1948. (U.N. Photo)

importance to us. The rest of the world is stunned. We have the power. We can act. We can try and understand our neighbors in this world."[19]

In the spring of 1946, the Bronx campus of Hunter served as the interim home of the United Nations. Mrs. Roosevelt was unanimously elected the first chair of the U.N.'s Human Rights Commission and she took charge of the commission's preparation of the Universal Declaration of Human Rights, which would be adopted by the U.N. General Assembly in December 1948. During the first meeting of the U.N. in its "makeshift quarters" at Hunter, there was a shortage of interpreters so Mrs. Roosevelt "conducted the commission's business alternately in French and English," relying on the fluency she had achieved while studying abroad during her youth.[20]

Even after Mrs. Roosevelt concluded her tenure with the United Nations, she continued to focus her attention on international relations in her Hunter College appearances. When the Metropolitan New York Council of the American Associations for the United Nations (AAUN) honored her at Hunter College in April 1953, she condemned groups such as the Daughters of the American Revolution that opposed the U.N.'s commitment to international cooperation.[21] A few days later, at the tenth anniversary of the dedication of Roosevelt House, she addressed the effect of the Cold War in creating divisions among young people in different countries. In 1955, as a volunteer with the AAUN, she discussed the U.N.'s role as a mediator in the Middle East: "Life has to be made worth living for both the Arab and Israeli people, for that is the only way in which peace will be achieved."[22]

Eleanor Roosevelt's last four appearances at college events came in 1960 and 1961. She honored the career of her friend and colleague, Hunter president George Shuster, on his retirement in January 1960. A few weeks later, she celebrated the college's ninetieth anniversary with a talk entitled "The Changing World and the Responsibility of Education." In March, she joined the college community in remembering the work of a kindred spirit, Adele Rosenwald Levy, late president of the Citizens Committee for Children of New York, for her philanthropy, civic leadership, championing of children and refugees, and patronage of the arts. "Everyone here knows," Eleanor said, "that the qualities she had were the qualities we need."[23] Finally, Eleanor and Senator Jacob Javits came to Hunter to talk about the Peace Corps in October 1961, just the kind of project that would nourish the international

*Eleanor Roosevelt maintained her political activities through-
out her life. Here she meets with Senator John F. Kennedy in
Massachusetts in January 1960. He knew that her support would
make his presidential bid stronger. (Courtesy of the Franklin D.
Roosevelt Library Digital Archives)*

understanding that was the foundation for peace and cultural
respect, long central to Eleanor's philosophy.

Regularly from 1940 to 1960, Eleanor met with Hunter
students informally. Shuster described her as "the only unpaid
member of the Hunter faculty," treasuring her many contributions
to college life.[24] Blanche Wiesen Cook, later Eleanor's biographer
and a professor at CUNY's John Jay College, attended Hunter
from 1958 to 1962 and served as president of the student government. Cook's memories of Mrs. Roosevelt convey her charisma:
"Each time the experience felt charged: the room simply changed
when she walked into it—one felt the air fill with her vibrancy.
. . . Eleanor Roosevelt was still, as she had been for decades, an

adviser to students—an optimistic galvanizing force for activism and political commitment."[25]

Hunter College continued to celebrate and sustain its ties with the Roosevelt family after Eleanor's death on November 7, 1962. On January 30, 1972, the Alumni Association commemorated the ninetieth birthday of Franklin Delano Roosevelt, raising funds for the upkeep of Roosevelt House with a symposium. FDR biographer Professor Arthur Schlesinger Jr. spoke on the former President's place in history, several Hunter faculty reflected on the President's role as a politician, internationalist, and molder of economic policy, and actress Ruby Dee (class of 1944) gave a reading from "The Man from Hyde Park."[26]

Two years later, on October 10, 1974, a tribute to Eleanor Roosevelt in the Hunter College Auditorium on the ninetieth anniversary of her birth was attended by more than 1,000 friends

Future Congresswoman Bella (Savitsky) Abzug, president of the class of 1942, sat on the dais with Eleanor Roosevelt during Eleanor's first speaking engagement at Hunter College in February 1941. Hunter president George Shuster was master of ceremonies. (Reva Fine Holtzman [Hunter College])

and family members, including her son Franklin Jr., daughter Anna Roosevelt Halsted, and grandchildren Eleanor Seagraves and Curtis Roosevelt. Dore Schary, author of the play *Sunrise at Campobello,* was master of ceremonies, actress Jane Alexander read scenes from *Eleanor,* a play by Jerome Coopersmith, and the audience listened to recordings of Eleanor while watching a montage of images and film. Congresswoman Bella Abzug, a 1942 graduate of Hunter, announced the designation of the day as an official national ceremony. In 1941, Abzug, then president of the student government, had met Eleanor and remembered "many of Mrs. Roosevelt's positions would get her cheers today from women's liberationists—she had the issues all figured out before the present generation was even worried about a mystique. Some of the credit

In October 1996, a statue of Eleanor Roosevelt was dedicated in Riverside Park at 72nd Street, the first woman so honored in the city's parks. The bronze figure was unveiled by then–First Lady Hillary Clinton.

Eleanor's spirit was now firmly anchored in the soil of New York City, where she had grown up and lived for so many years as a good friend of Hunter College and as a revered and beloved citizen of the world. (New York City Parks Department)

for our movement belongs to Eleanor Roosevelt who was there before us and will always be with us in spirit."[27]

In December 1982, Hunter College hosted the First Lady Conference, organized by Professor Barbara Welter, a women's studies scholar, and by Joseph Lash, a longtime associate of Eleanor Roosevelt and author of *Eleanor and Franklin*. More than 800 people attended to learn about the evolving role of the First Lady and, in particular, about the pragmatic and idealistic qualities of Eleanor that served her so well in that role. One of the key speakers, Justine Wise Polier, was chair of the Eleanor Roosevelt Institute. The first woman judge in New York State, Polier had taken a leave in 1941 to serve as Special Council to Mrs. Roosevelt at the Office of Civilian Defense. Eleanor Roosevelt had "an inner core that was untouchable, indestructible," Polier said. "Her life became part of history."[28]

◆

ENDNOTES

1   "Roosevelt To Tour 5 Boroughs Today," *New York Times*, October 28, 1940, 1, 8.
2   "Hunter Dedicates 16-Story Building," *New York Times*, October 9, 1940, 27.
3   "Need for Guidance of Youth Stressed," *New York Times*, October 29, 1940, 13.
4   Trinsey, *College Bulletin*, speaking on January 30, 1972 on the occasion of the Hunter College Alumni Association's celebration of the 90th birthday of Eleanor Roosevelt.
5   Marian Shomer Greene, "My Brush With History. Lonely (First) Lady," *American Heritage* 51 no. 6 (October 2000): 26.
6   "Need for Guidance of Youth Stressed," *New York Times*, October 29, 1940, 13.
7   Greene, "My Brush With History," 25.
8   "My Day, " May 30, 1942; Naomi Block Stern Manners Collection of Eleanor Roosevelt Correspondence, Center for Jewish History, http://digital.cjh.org; "Hunter Junior Heads Student Government," *New York Times*, May 13, 1941, 19.
9   Shuster, "An Autobiography," 27. Shuster was acting president from fall 1939 to fall 1940 and was inducted as president in October 1940.
10 "First Lady to Speak," *New York Times*, February 9, 1941, D6.
11 E. Adelaide Hahn, "Mrs. Roosevelt's Visit," *Alumnae News*, March 1941, 1–4.
12 For full text of Franklin Delano Roosevelt, Executive Order 8802, June 25, 1941,

see Our Documents, Franklin Delano Roosevelt Presidential Library. http://docs.fdrlibrary.marist.edu.

13 Hahn, "Mrs. Roosevelt's Visit," 1–4

14 Hahn, "Mrs. Roosevelt's Visit," 4; Rose C. Goldberg [Class of 1941], "First Lady in Her Own Right," *Echo* (March 1941), 4.

15 "Homes of President and Mother To Be Hunter Community House," *New York Times*, June 25, 1942, 1, 18. The outline for Eleanor Roosevelt's talk can be found in FDR Library, Eleanor Roosevelt Papers, Box 3045, Hunter College Commencement, June 24, 1942. FDR's "four essential human freedoms" were freedom of speech and expression, freedom of religion, freedom from want, and freedom from fear.

16 "My Day, " June 26, 1942, Eleanor Roosevelt Papers Project, http://www.gwu.edu/~erpapers/myday/.

17 "My Day," May 30, 1942, Eleanor Roosevelt Papers Project, http://www.gwu.edu/~erpapers/myday/.

18 "My Day," April 18, 1944, Eleanor Roosevelt Papers Project, http://www.gwu.edu/~erpapers/myday/.

19 "Plea for UNO Made By Mrs. Roosevelt," *New York Times*, February 28, 1946, 3.

20 "U.N. Group Honors Mrs. Roosevelt," *New York Times*, March 11, 1961, 3, and "U.N. Group Headed By Mrs. Roosevelt," *New York Times*, April 30, 1946, 9. Mrs. Roosevelt was also selected as an ex-officio member of the Commission's sub-commission on the status of women.

21 "D.A.R. Stand on U.N. Scored," *New York Times*, April 25, 1953.

22 "U.N. Policing Urged by Mrs. Roosevelt," *New York Times*, May 21, 1955, 19.

23 "Governor, Mayor Praise Mrs. Levy," *New York Times*, March 19, 1960, 21.

24 Blantz, *Shuster*, 193.

25 Blanche Wiesen Cook, *Eleanor Roosevelt*, Vol. 1, (New York: Viking, 1992), xi–xii.

26 Program of the 90th birthday celebration.

27 "Mrs. Roosevelt Memorial To Be Held at Hunter," *New York Times*, October 10, 1974, 53; "Eleanor Roosevelt Honored at Hunter," *New York Times*, October 11, 1974, 41; Program of the 90th birthday celebration.

28 "A Conference Report – First Ladies," *Hunter Magazine*, March 1983, 11.

◆ APPENDIX ONE ◆
SELECTED BIBLIOGRAPHY

BOOKS

Asbell, Bernard. *Mother & Daughter: the Letters of Eleanor and Anna Roosevelt.* New York: Coward, McCann & Geoghegan, 1982.

Black, Conrad. *Franklin Delano Roosevelt: Champion of Freedom.* New York: Perseus Publishing, 2003.

Blantz, Thomas E., C.S.C. *George N. Shuster – On the Side of Truth.* Notre Dame, IN: University of Notre Dame Press, 1993.

Burns, James MacGregor and Susan Dunn. *The Three Roosevelts: Patrician Leaders Who Transformed America.* New York: Atlantic Monthly Press, 2001.

Caroli, Betty Boyd. *The Roosevelt Women: A Portrait in Five Generations.* New York: Basic Books, 1998.

Cook, Blanche Wiesen. *Eleanor Roosevelt.* Volume 1, 1884 –1933. New York: Viking Penguin, 1992.

Cook, Blanche Wiesen. *Eleanor Roosevelt, The Defining Years.* Volume 2, 1933–38. New York: Viking Penguin, 1999.

Davis, Kenneth S. *FDR: The Beckoning of Destiny, 1882–1928.* New York: G.P. Putnam's Sons, 1972–91.

———. *FDR: The New York Years, 1928–1933.* New York: Random House, 1985.

———. *FDR: Into the Storm, 1937–1940 A History.* New York: Random House, 1993.

Donn, Linda. *The Roosevelt Cousins: Growing Up Together, 1882–1924.* New York: Alfred A. Knopf, 2001.

Downey, Kristin. *The Woman Behind the New Deal: The Life of Frances Perkins, FDR's Secretary of Labor and His Moral Conscience.* New York: Doubleday, 2009.

Ellis, Francis M. and Edward F. Clark Jr. *A Brief History of Carter, Ledyard & Milburn, from 1854–1988.* New York: Carter, Ledyard & Milburn, 1988.

Evans, Hugh E. *The Hidden Campaign: FDR's Health and the 1944 Campaign.* Armonk, NY: M.E. Sharpe, 2002.

Hoff-Wilson, Joan and Marjorie Lightman, eds. *Without Precedent: The Life and Career of Eleanor Roosevelt.* Bloomington: Indiana University Press, 1984.

Jackson, Robert H. *That Man. An Insider's Portrait of Franklin D. Roosevelt.* Edited and Introduced by John Q. Barrett. New York: Oxford University Press, 2003.

Lannie, Vincent P., ed. *On the Side of Truth: George N. Shuster, an Evaluation with Readings.* South Bend, IN: University of Notre Dame Press, 1974.

Lash, Joseph P. *Eleanor and Franklin.* New York: Norton, 1971.

————. *Eleanor: The Years Alone.* New York: Norton, 1972.

Morgan, Keith N. *Charles A. Platt: The Artist as Architect.* Cambridge, MA and New York: M.I.T. Press and The Architectural History Foundation, 1985.

Morgan, Keith N., et al. *Shaping an American Landscape: The Art and Architecture of Charles A. Platt.* Hanover, NH: University Press of New England and Hood Museum of Art, 1995.

Pottker, Jan. *Sara and Eleanor. The Story of Sara Delano Roosevelt and Her Daughter-in-Law, Eleanor Roosevelt.* New York: St. Martin's Press, 2004.

Rollins, Alfred B., Jr. *Roosevelt and Howe.* New York: Alfred A. Knopf, 1962.

Roosevelt, Curtis. *Too Close to the Sun: Growing Up in the Shadow of My Grandparents, Franklin and Eleanor.* New York: Public Affairs, 2008.

Roosevelt, David B. with Manuela Dunn Mascetti. *Grandmere: A Personal History of Eleanor Roosevelt.* New York: Warner Books, 2002.

Roosevelt, Eleanor. *This Is My Story.* New York: Harper & Brothers, 1937.

————. *This I Remember.* New York: Harper & Brothers, 1949.

————. *The Autobiography of Eleanor Roosevelt.* New York: HarperCollins, 1961 (orig.); Da Capo Press, 1992.

Roosevelt, Elliott and James Brough. *An Untold Story: The Roosevelts of Hyde Park.* New York: G.P. Putnam's Sons, 1973.

[Roosevelt, Sara Delano] Mrs. James Roosevelt as told to Isabel Leighton and Gabrielle Forbush. *My Boy Franklin.* New York: Ray Long & Richard R. Smith, 1933.

Rosenman, Samuel I. *Working with Roosevelt*. New York: Harper & Brothers, 1952.

Ward, Geoffrey C. *A First-Class Temperament: The Emergence of Franklin Roosevelt*. New York: HarperCollins, 1989.

Ward, Geoffrey C., editor and annotator. *Closest Companion: The Unknown Story of the Intimate Friendship between Franklin Roosevelt and Margaret Suckley*. Boston: Houghton Mifflin Company, 1995.

ARCHIVES AND COLLECTIONS

Franklin Delano Roosevelt Library and Museum, Hyde Park, N.Y.

March of Dimes Archives

Eleanor Roosevelt Papers Project at The George Washington University, http://www.gwu.edu/~erpapers/

Hunter College Archives & Special Collections

REPORTS

Sara Delano Roosevelt Memorial House Designation Report. New York: New York City Landmarks Preservation Commission, September 25, 1973.

Upper East Side Historic Designation Report, vol. 1. New York: New York City Landmarks Preservation Commission, 1981.

Murray Hill Historic District Extensions Report. New York: New York City Landmarks Preservation Commission, March 30, 2004.

ARTICLES, NEWSPAPERS, MAGAZINES, AND WEBSITES

Georgia Info. "FDR's Ties to Georgia." Available at http://georgiainfo.galileo.usg.edu/FDRtitle.htm.

Gray, Christopher. "The Roosevelt Townhouse 47–49 East 65th Street." *Kips Bay Boys and Girls Club Decorator Show Program* (April–May 1994): 71–73.

Kroessler, Jeffrey A. "Eleanor Roosevelt and Hunter College." Paper presented at the conference, "The Vision of Eleanor Roosevelt: World Citizen Ahead of Her Time," at Hofstra University, September 30–October 2, 1999. The story of Hunter College and Roosevelt House, and Hunter College and the Roosevelts, was first laid out in this paper.

Minster, Emma Lou. "The Home of the President's Mother." *Ladies Home Journal* (April 1934): 12, 13, 95.

The New York Times Historical, 1851–2006 (Proquest Historical Newspapers) accessed online. A complete list of articles consulted are available in an annotated version of this history available at the website of the Roosevelt House Public Policy Institute (www.roosevelthouse. hunter.cuny.edu).

Perkins, Linda M. "African-American Women and Hunter College: 1873–1945." *The ECHO, Journal of the Hunter College Archives* (1995): 22–23.

Roosevelt, Eleanor. "I Remember Hyde Park: A Final Reminiscence." posthumous. *McCall's* February 1963: 73.

Roosevelt, Eleanor. "My Day," nationally syndicated newspaper column (December 30, 1935–September 27, 1962). Available at http://www. gwu.edu/~erpapers/.

"Susie Parish." Eleanor Roosevelt National Historic Site. Available at http://www.nps.gov/elro/glossary/parish_susie.htm.

The full manuscript on which this book is based, "Roosevelt House: Historic Structure Report," is available on the website of the Roosevelt House Public Policy Institute at www.roosevelthouse.hunter.cuny.edu.

ACKNOWLEDGEMENTS

I am grateful for the assistance of a number of people and organizations in the preparation of this essay. The starting point was Jennifer Raab's inspired vision to renovate the house, which required documenting its history and the relationship of the Roosevelts to Hunter. Administrative and research support at Hunter came from Provost Vita Rabinowitz, Fay Rosenfeld, Ellen Murray, Danielle Cylich, and Hunter Archivist Professor Julio L. Hernandez-Delgado. Photography assistance was provided by Evgenia Gennadiou and Ashley Hartka. David Rose of the March of Dimes Archives, staff at the FDR Library and Museum, and historians Blanche Cook, Christine McKay, and Glenna Matthews also contributed to shaping this work. Jeffrey Kroessler's original work on Eleanor Roosevelt and Hunter College laid the groundwork for my efforts. Finally, I honor my parents who raised me in a household that revered the Roosevelts and created my life-long interest, and my husband and daughter who accompanied me on the Roosevelt trail from Campobello to Warm Springs and beyond over the last few years.

DEBORAH S. GARDNER

◆ APPENDIX TWO ◆
PRESIDENTIAL HOMES IN
NEW YORK CITY

Roosevelt House is the only former residence of a United States president in New York City that is the original structure, maintains its historic integrity, and is open to the public. The following men lived in New York City before, during, or after their presidential terms.

Washington

GEORGE WASHINGTON (1732–1799) was president from 1789 to 1797. He lived in New York City in 1776 while commanding the Continental Army against the British; the Mortier House on Charlton Street between Varick and MacDougal Streets, where he had his headquarters, is no longer extant. When he took the presidential oath of office on April 30, 1789 in the City Hall at the corner of Wall and Broad Streets, he lived at 39 Broadway, which also no longer exists. Seven months later, the federal government moved to Philadelphia.

ULYSSES S. GRANT (1822–1885) was president from 1869 to 1877. In retirement he lived at 3 East 66th Street (no longer extant) from August 1881 to his death in July 1885. He and his wife are interred within Grant's Tomb, a national memorial overlooking the Hudson River at Riverside Drive and West 122nd Street.

Grant, 1865

CHESTER A. ARTHUR (1829–1886) bought a brownstone at 123 Lexington Avenue between 28th and 29th Streets in 1860. He was elected vice president in 1880, and succeeded James Garfield as president on September 20, 1881, after Garfield died of wounds received from an assassin. Arthur took the oath of office at 123 Lexington. He returned to this home in the spring of 1885 where he lived until his death on November 18, 1886. The building still exists, its exterior more or less intact, with a store on the ground floor and second floor, and apartments above, but it is not open to the public and has only a plaque to record its place in history.

Arthur, c. 1882

THEODORE ROOSEVELT (1852–1919) was president from 1901 to 1909. He was born at 28 East 20th Street, a brownstone constructed in 1848, and lived there until 1866. The house was demolished in 1916. After Roosevelt died, the Women's Roosevelt Memorial Association raised funds to rebuild the house and create a museum with family furnishings. The Theodore Roosevelt Birthplace National Historic Site is a replica built in 1923 to designs by architect Theodate Pope Riddle.

Roosevelt, c. 1904

HERBERT HOOVER (1874–1964) was president from 1929 to 1933. He lived at the Waldorf Towers, part of the Waldorf-Astoria Hotel at 301 Park Avenue at 50th Street, from 1934 until his death in 1964.

Hoover, no date

JOHN F. KENNEDY (1917–1963) was president from 1961 to 1963. He lived in the Riverdale

section of the Bronx as a child from 1927
to 1929 in a home at 252nd Street and
Independence Avenue. The family then lived
in Bronxville, N.Y. in Westchester County until
1942. Kennedy's widow, Jacqueline Kennedy,
maintained an apartment in Manhattan until
her own death in 1994.

Kennedy, c. 1961

Nixon, c. 1970

RICHARD NIXON (1913–1994) was president
from 1969 to 1974. He lived in an apartment at 810 Fifth Avenue from 1963 until
his election as president in 1968. In 1979,
he bought a row house on East 65th Street,
the former home of Judge Billings Learned
Hand, but sold it in 1982.